Working at a Distance

Working at a Distance

A Global Business Model for Virtual Team Collaboration

CASSANDRA J. SMITH

Routledge
Taylor & Francis Group

LONDON AND NEW YORK

First published 2014 by Gower Publishing

Published 2016 by Routledge
2 Park Square, Milton Park, Abingdon, Oxfordshire OX14 4RN
711 Third Avenue, New York, NY 10017, USA

First issued in paperback 2016

Routledge is an imprint of the Taylor & Francis Group, an informa business

Gower Applied Business Research
Our programme provides leaders, practitioners, scholars and researchers with thought
provoking, cutting edge books that combine conceptual insights, interdisciplinary
rigour and practical relevance in key areas of business and management.

British Library Cataloguing in Publication Data
A catalogue record for this book is available from the British Library.

Library of Congress Cataloging-in-Publication Data
Smith, Cassandra J.
    Working at a distance : a global business model for virtual team collaboration / by
Cassandra J. Smith.
        pages cm
    Includes bibliographical references and index.
    ISBN 978-1-4724-2523-2 (hardback : alk. paper)
    1. Virtual reality in management. 2. Virtual work teams—Management. I. Title.
    HD30.2122.S65 2014
    658.4′022—dc23

                                                                        2013042240

ISBN 13: 978-1-138-25032-1 (pbk)
ISBN 13: 978-1-4724-2523-2 (hbk)

CONTENTS

LIST OF FIGURES AND TABLES

FIGURES

TABLES

ABOUT THE AUTHOR

Cassandra Smith is an online instructor. She has been writing for over twenty years, and teaching in the online environment for six years. She has taught several courses online and facilitated a number of virtual teams. She has also designed Web-based courses and trained online faculty. She is the author of the course guide for online facilitators *Who Let this Disaster in My Classroom? A Practical Guide for Online Instructors and Some Funny Stories Along the Way* (2009) and *Ethical Behaviour in the E-Classroom: What the Online Student Needs to Know* (2012), a textbook for online students featuring ethical theories as they relate to working in the online environment along with critical thinking concepts. She holds a Bachelor of Science degree in Communication from the University of Mobile and a Master of Arts in Education with an emphasis on Adult Education and Distance Learning from the University of Phoenix. She is currently a doctoral candidate in the Postsecondary and Adult Education discipline.

ACKNOWLEDGMENTS

The idea of writing a book about virtual teams came about as a result of working in and facilitating them. My experiences with students and as a student led to my research on how to manage virtual teams more effectively. It is my hope that this book will serve as a guide to virtual team development for business professionals and those working in higher education.

I would like to thank God for all my ideas and purpose in life. I want to thank my husband for his continuous support and consistent spiritual guidance and love. I want to thank my mother, father, siblings, nephews, and family. Their support and love have been the catalyst for me to meet my goals. I love you.

To Gower Publishing—I want to express my sincere gratitude for accepting this book. You are a true leader in the business and education industry.

To my students—you helped me grow. I pray that I have been an excellent instructor and example of the importance of lifelong learning.

REVIEWS OF *WORKING AT A DISTANCE*

"Many projects fail in the virtual environment because project managers rely on the assumptions and communication strategies they use in the face-to-face environment. Smith's Virtual Team Global Business Model makes a significant contribution to working and learning at a distance because she provides a concrete model that helps managers examine their assumptions and tailor their communication practices to work effectively at a distance."

Howard R. Jacobs, School of Education, Capella University, USA

"Cassandra Smith's Virtual Team Global Business Model™ is a methodology that can finally make virtual teamwork viable. Through her thoughtful and creative structuring of goal-planning, role-definition, communication, and much more, Smith paints a multifaceted picture of how this business process can work in higher education. We no longer should hear, 'oh, no, not another team assignment!'"

Tamara Fudge, Kaplan University, USA

INTRODUCING THE VIRTUAL TEAM GLOBAL BUSINESS MODEL

As a manager, you have established your goals and objectives for your employees working at a distance—in virtual teams—with their coworkers. You are certain that your expectations are clear. You have submitted the expectations to your employees in the form of statements with the end goal in mind—your mind. Your deliverable due dates are set in place as well, and you expect your employees to submit project deliverables by due dates. You believe that your employees working collaboratively understand the Web-based technology required to submit the deliverables. You believe that your employees understand how to communicate in their teams. You reason that your employees know how to use email and any real-time platforms that your company uses to communicate. All systems are set in place and ready for completion of the project.

But consider this scenario—a distance project—from the perspectives of your employees working at a distance: there is a project due, and your employer has assigned you to work with others to complete the project. This sounds like a simple feat. The issue is that you are not in the same location as your counterparts, your team members, your peers. You are working at a distance, assigned to a virtual team. You might be wondering where to begin. You have no guidelines or set rules. The goals and objectives are ambiguous to you and read like a list of commands, not clear steps on how to proceed. You might have initiated contact with some of your team members by email, only to find that only a few members have responded. One member has informed you that he prefers to use Skype, so please Skype him.

You wonder to yourself, "Is this indicative of how effective the team will progress?" You have a myriad of questions. Since you initiated the email, are you now considered the team leader, the go-to person? Will there be a team leader? Where are management? Should you approach management about how to move forward? Will that make it look like you're not a competent employee who understands remote working?

This book was developed to help professionals and participants in higher education working at a distance in what are known as virtual teams. Virtual teams occur when groups that are geographically dispersed work together using Web technologies to complete projects. Virtual teams facilitate work that occurs across diverse and disseminated areas and business centers; some virtual teams are in offices throughout the country and globally for businesses; some virtual teams are in employees' home offices. Universities also find virtual teams useful as they are part of curricula to foster collaborative learning among students.

As noted above, virtual teams consist of groups of individuals working at a distance to complete a project or meet an identified common goal. Working at a distance could consist of asynchronous or synchronous communication, depending on the organization and strategic goals set by stakeholders for the organization. The premise of this book is to introduce a model that can be applied and followed when working collaboratively on projects challenged by distance. It is not always an easy task to work on projects and have a grasp of the skills needed for the job, to be in the know regarding which subgroups within the team will complete project parts, and to be fully aware of how to overcome communication barriers due to using technology mostly to communicate. These are among the factors that play a significant role in determining whether or not virtual teams will result in success. When employees have a guide and standards regarding how to work remotely, they are motivated to work collaboratively and submit quality work.

Before reviewing the details of this marvelous model, how it works, how it can be applied, and how it is set up to meet your distance work demands for remote projects, it is important to introduce some elements of virtual teams and virtual team dynamics that will be discussed throughout the book. Keep in mind that this chapter is a preview of the entire book, of what is to come, and poses salient questions that will be answered later.

ASYNCHRONOUS COMMUNICATION

Asynchronous communication involves participants working at a distance at their own pace, their own computer terminals, and sometimes at home. Participants can log on to their computers to independently complete tasks for the group project that have been assigned to a particular individual or that the individual has volunteered to complete. Some online schools use virtual teams in an asynchronous format. Students have a project due, and work in class posting messages (threads) about the assignment section they will complete, and then submit their sections of the assignment. Virtual teams in higher education will be discussed in more detail in Chapter 6.

Asynchronous communication tools include the following:

- **email**—participants may submit work using their companies' email software;
- **newsgroups**—participants may submit their work by communicating in a particular area of the Internet provided by the company known as a newsgroup to organize projects and tasks;
- **distance education software**—participants may submit their work via software, using educational tools specially designed for Web-based learning such as Pearson eCollege or Blackboard Learning System.

Issues that occur in asynchronous virtual teams include lack of communication and miscommunication. Reading an email alone or working in an area of software dedicated to team participation is not always effective. The communication is asynchronous, which means that employees, students, or any participants working at a distance can log on to work whenever they choose. There are no set times to communicate and work as a group. When one person responds to an email, it could be nighttime in another location. This can lead to increasing miscommunication and slow team progress.

Other issues that occur in asynchronous communication involve technology. Managers may assume that employees can work effectively with the technology to collaborate within an asynchronous group. Participants themselves may assume that they understand the technology until it is time to work. There may be delays in the submission of deliverables because there is no central point to submit the work to or the employee cannot locate the central point or area for updates. Often, these are thought to be secondary issues that are not resolved until the project is under way, when in fact they should be a priority because they impact the delivery of products and services.

SYNCHRONOUS COMMUNICATION

Synchronous communication involves participants working at a distance as a group at the same time. Participants take part in synchronous communication by using videoconferencing or Web-based technologies that allow working at a distance simultaneously. Although this book focuses mostly on asynchronous teams, synchronous virtual teams may benefit from it as well. Synchronous teams work on projects using technologies that provide participants with the opportunity for face-to-face communication. Synchronous communication tools include the following:

- **videoconferencing**—video and audio telecommunication for collaborative work;
- **conference calls**—telecommunication by telephone with audio capabilities to share ideas;
- **Webconferencing**—real-time chat, video, and audio capabilities using software systems such as Adobe Connect or Cisco WebEx.

Issues that result from synchronous communication usually include a few people doing the speaking and not enough listening to employees by management and/or not enough active engagement from all employees. The chat feature involves numerous participants asking questions with limited answers from the host. Participants can easily become discouraged about the size of the meetings, their voice not being heard, or their ideas not being fully or accurately represented, or failing to participate and offer ideas. Some participants are reticent in these types of settings, while others are more forthcoming and will express themselves to the team. For either group—asynchronous or synchronous—there is usually no evaluation component in place enabling management and participants to determine and review what is working and what is not working in virtual teams.

Once the communication tools are set in place, participants can work either with asynchronous, synchronous, or both types of communications to meet virtual team goals. Members are given tasks, time limits to complete the tasks, perhaps some goals and objectives, and then expectations for deliverables. The deliverables are the actual product, assignment, or service that participants are working to complete. The problem is that there are often performance gaps in communication between the task allocated and the deliverables expected. Providing a model for remote workers to follow allows each member of the team to clearly understand their role.

PERFORMANCE GAPS

"Performance gap" is a business term meaning that some part of a task is disjointed or not connected to meet an intended goal. The gap is between where the company is currently operating and where it should be operating. For businesses, it may mean that a more strategic approach is needed to close the performance gap and achieve goals. For virtual teamwork, it means that there is no clarity and limited action steps are occurring because somewhere there is miscommunication, a gap, and slow progression. Here is an example involving O-Span Youth, a fictitious company that will be used to illustrate the methodology throughout this book.

O-Span Youth, a children's shoe company, has noticed that there is a gap in shoe sales and wants to devise an advertising campaign in the hope of selling more shoes. Its management want several of its subsidiary companies to work on the campaign across its Northeast region. The gap currently consists of the low levels of sales management have identified. Future gaps could include communication among the geographically dispersed teams working to complete the campaign, among other issues that may ensue if there are no set rules and protocols for this virtual assignment.

Performance gaps can be minimized if there are process standards to follow. The model introduced in this book allows for management and leaders to define process standards to help overcome performance gaps. Later in the book we will discuss process standards, and the example of O-Span Youth will be used to demonstrate how such a model can be effective for remote working.

GOALS AND OBJECTIVES

If management are initially involved in setting up the virtual team project, they need to be fully present and connected to the project. In this book, goals and objectives, tasks, and expectations for deliverables are some of the main areas of management involvement that will be discussed. These particular areas help to sustain virtual team collaboration. Goals are defined by management, and subsequent goals often follow when the participants start to work on their assigned projects. For example, a goal could be to design demographic software for the children's shoe company, but the objectives could be obscure, postulated by management, therefore leading to a performance gap at an early stage. If management fail to communicate the demographics they want included in the software and to connect the objectives to the goals, the miscommunication has begun, and will extend to the employees working at a distance. The team working on developing the demographic software—the actual design—will have to ask the management team what is needed with regard to standard operating procedures, or it may decide to design the software based on members' areas of expertise, including the demographics that are standard and that they think need to be included. This is where a subject matter expert would be helpful. But was a subject matter expert consulted? One designer might think the goals and objectives consist of a demographic that includes female, male, age, and location. A subject matter expert might include culture, assess prior market sales, surplus, and so on.

If you are assessing the flow thus far, you may notice an emerging theme of miscommunication from the start of the virtual team project or any project that requires group collaboration.

TASKS

Tasks are easy to identify, especially by stakeholders. Usually, management understand what they want to do and the desired end product. Management know that they want to increase sales of the children's shoes. They understand that the tasks will require employees working in satellite locations to achieve this goal. The task is clearly defined, at least from management's viewpoint, but the performance gap for this project may be subtle yet present. Tasks should result in specific steps of action needed regarding what is expected from employees' job performance on the virtual team. Nowhere has this been identified at this point. Management have really identified the goal, not the task.

EXPECTATIONS OF DELIVERABLES

Expectations of deliverables often conflict when working at a distance. What management and leadership teams want in terms of project quality may be radically different from what employees are working to complete or submit. The performance gap may be wide because there is often a lack of communication and clear expectations of management's goals regarding employees' final deliverables when working remotely. Not only are the tangible deliverables questionable, but the timeline and what each employee should be working on to complete the project factor into expectations of deliverables. As stated above, deliverables are the tangible evidence that shows work is being completed, and completed in the way that is desired. Some employees will not meet deadlines. The reasons may include difference in work ethic, performance gap issues, miscommunication, and uncertainty about project goals and objectives. If the performance gap includes issues with what is actually desired as opposed to what is submitted, deliverables may be delayed. Completing the task will be problematic because of previous performance gaps. Employees may in fact produce deliverables, but there may be reliability issues with the end products because of problems or delays in production to complete tasks due to having to go back and close the performance gaps.

CHECK-POINTS

There is one more element of virtual team dynamics that needs to be previewed before the grand introduction of the model: check-points. Between the lines of communication in cyberspace, there is a huge disconnect. That disconnect is as nebulous as the expression "between the lines of communication". Think about it. When there are updates and changes in a face-to-face environment on a huge project, how often are you updated, regardless of whether you are in management or an employee? Is there a sense of immediacy to check an update if you are notified by email, for instance? A lack of check-points and communication of changes that may be made on a whim or during a live testing event of products by management/employees means that they may never be conveyed to all staff or in the operating procedure manuals accurately, if at all, because these changes have not been fully captured. These intricacies impact the overall goals of the project and communication among employees. This occurs even in traditional teams, so what might happen in virtual teams where there may be no sense of urgency and no check-points for communication among employees working remotely?

INTRODUCING THE VIRTUAL TEAM GLOBAL BUSINESS MODEL™ (VTML)

Having collected empirical data, it seems that more and more companies are using technologies to work at a distance and bring employees together, and higher education establishments are using them to allow students who are often not in the same location to collaborate on projects. With a significant number of professionals working at a distance in the workforce, a viable plan for effective collaboration will not only help to integrate virtual teams seamlessly, but will provide guidance for those who have not yet experienced working in virtual teams or who are not prepared to meet the challenges of collaborating at a distance in the workforce or in higher education. This book introduces the Virtual Team Global Business Model™ for professionals who are developing or facilitating virtual teams, and those working (collaboratively) at a distance in virtual teams. We will discuss topics that are pivotal to the success of virtual teams and working collaboratively.

ADULT PROFESSIONALS ON VIRTUAL TEAMS

In August of 2012, 316 adult professionals were surveyed on whether they had worked in virtual teams: 73% said that they had experienced working in virtual teams, while 27% said that they hadn't.

As a manager, asking the specific questions below can help you to assess the importance of the VTML for your employees or participants working at a distance. As explained in the introductory scenario, you may assume that your instructions to your employees are clear and that they understand how to move forward with their own and their counterparts' responsibilities in the team project. However, that might not be the reality of remote working on distance projects. Using the

VTML, goals and objectives are defined with *precise* steps, reducing the gap between assumptions and facts. If managers are active in the initial stages of planning a group task, employees will be clear about how to move forward and what their expected deliverables are. Consider the following questions about your virtual teams.

Question 1: Why the need for a Virtual Team Global Business Model?

The need for a Virtual Team Global Business Model ranges from management communication with employees to employees understanding how to work effectively at a distance. It is global in the sense that employees in dispersed locations working together can use it as guide for expectations when submitting deliverables (assigned parts of project) and a foundation for communication. All outstanding projects, products, assignments, and tasks are underpinned by clear communication and skills. In the introductory scenario, management assumed that they had conveyed clear expectations and goals for the project, but there were no defined tasks, no communication plans, and no accountability—a surefire recipe for poor communication when working at a distance. The VTML ensures that all processes are in place for top-level collaborative project performance.

Question 2: Are your Virtual Team Projects object-driven or people-driven?

Have you assumed that your employees will understand how to use technology to communicate about the task assigned, bridge any gaps due to response time, and understand their responsibilities for the project? If you are an object-driven manager, you may assume the technology will do the work. You may expect employees to be familiar with the software used to work at a distance, such as email and Web-based technologies, and to be able to resolve the metamessages that often accompany online correspondence. If you are a people-driven manager, you may feel that although your employees are using technology as the vehicle to submit projects and communicate, they still need to communicate verbally; there has to be some component of audible communication. If you are a people-driven as manager, you may also understand the need for employees working at a distance to have assigned responsibilities for projects, to have specific, clear guidelines and realistic due dates, to take on active roles and check in consistently with their virtual team coworkers; as a people-driven manager, you may understand that employees need to have meetings that allow their voices to be heard and opportunities that allow them to present ideas as well as discuss any challenges.

Question 3: Do you have an established hierarchical Virtual Team Network with clear communication?

Another area to be mindful of as you work to develop collaborative projects for your employees and participants working remotely is that there should be a hierarchical process for working at a distance to ensure clear communication. Notice that in all three questions so far, a consistent theme is communication. Without efficient communication, the gap of miscommunication may be too wide, especially when working online. Revisiting the introductory scenario from the employee's perspective, the employee is reaching out to colleagues hoping that they will respond or hoping to generate some ideas. Brainstorming is good for generating ideas and pre-planning for projects. However, if employees are inactive with no set ground rules or no accountability to anyone through checks and balances, the project can quickly go awry, resulting in delayed or unintended project outcomes. The virtual team project may not be prioritized. Some employees may very well have the mindset that if management doesn't care about what is occurring on the teams, why should they, as employees, care?

Question 4: Do you assume that your Virtual Team employees understand process standards?

For those working at a distance, understanding process standards depends on management defining them. Process standards encompass communication as well. They can be an aspect of creating objectives for projects, and most importantly, defining tasks that employees should complete within the team. Process standards cover employees working autonomously on assigned tasks for the group, working collaboratively, group problem solving, evaluation, and results. Process standards are guidelines, and are often value-based with levels of expectancy. Process standards as they apply to the VTML will be discussed in more detail in Chapter 5. If employees are not fully aware of process standards, an array of issues in virtual team collaboration could result.

Question 5: Is your overall Virtual Team Project/communication structure substandard?

This question can be answered with an emphatic yes or no. Substandard is below average, and a below-average product on the market usually does not bode well financially for the company or for its reputation.

Next, ponder this final question carefully.

Question 6: As a manager, have you left your virtual team employees to figure out for themselves how to work at a distance, assuming that they understand objectives and your expectations for work projects?

If so, the Virtual Team Global Business Model is for you and your organization.

BENEFITS OF THE VIRTUAL TEAM GLOBAL BUSINESS MODEL

The questions posed above were intended to provide a business self-assessment of where you might need help and support regarding working at a distance with your virtual team of participants. Participants can include any, more, or all of the following people who work collaboratively in a geographically dispersed way: employers, employees, managers, assistants, students, instructors, and vendors. The benefits of having the VTML as a guide are as follows:

- It provides a hierarchal process for distance teamwork.
- It specifies a clear communication process.
- It helps to define process standards.
- It sets clear goals, objectives, and tasks for participants.
- It solidifies the expected deliverables for remote workers.
- It can be used along with distance working software.

Table 1.1   Definitions of terms used in the Virtual Team Global Business Model

Term	Definition
Communication flow	Electronic communication flow, including the electronic message itself, the technology conveying it, metamessages, acknowledgement and interpretation
Communication Phase 1	The first phase in the VTML, consisting of synchronous meetings between management and team leaders or project managers to allow management to explain goals, objectives, tasks, and timelines
Communication Phase 2	The second phase in the VTML, consisting of synchronous meetings between team leaders or project managers, virtual team guides, and virtual team members to review expected deliverables
Communication Phase 3	The third phase in the VTML, consisting of synchronous meetings between team leaders or project managers, virtual team guides, and virtual team members to conduct an open assessment of deliverables, and possibly the testing of deliverables
Critical thinking	A fair and balanced thinking process that aids in decision making and understanding others' perspectives when working remotely
Deliverables	Tangible or intangible items that signify that the goals have been met
Goals	Statements that explain desired outcomes for a project

Table 1.1   Definitions of terms used in the Virtual Team Global Business Model *continued*

Term	Definition
Instructional designers (ISDs)	Course creators responsible for developing subject content for students working remotely, especially in higher education
Management	A person or group of persons responsible for initiating the remote project; in the VTML, management are responsible for developing goals, objectives and tasks
Metamessages	Nonverbal messages that affect the way a message is perceived by the receiver that may or may not be accurate or intended by the sender
Objectives	A preview of responsibilities executed by virtual team members that will support the goals
O-Span Youth	A fictitious children's shoe company used to illustrate the VTML throughout this book
Process standards	Guidelines to be met during project development that reinforce the company's standards, mission and reputation
Project manager	A person or group of persons responsible for driving the remote project; project managers are responsible for ensuring that deliverables are consistent with process standards
Project needs	The essentials of project development
Remote check-in	Meetings, asynchronous or synchronous, that allow the virtual team guide to receive updates and stay in contact with virtual team members to offer support
Synergy	A community of VTML members working in harmony with consistent interaction and engagement with support from strong, present leadership
Tasks	Specific steps derived from the objectives that virtual team members must complete to meet deliverable expectations
Team leader	A person or group of persons responsible for overseeing the remote project; team leaders, like project managers, are responsible for ensuring that deliverables are consistent with process standards

Term	Definition
Virtual Team Global Business Model (VTML)	A framework created for virtual teams and/or professionals working remotely on projects to follow to promote clear communication, desired expectations, and a hierarchal process of accountability among management, leaders, virtual team guides, and virtual team members, leading to outstanding projects
Virtual team guide (VTG)	A person or group of persons skilled in communication and conflict strategies for remote working; VTGs are responsible for facilitating and helping virtual team members meet deliverable expectations
Virtual team in higher education (VTHE)	A team project that includes geographically dispersed students working collaboratively on a project to achieve a grade
Virtual team member (VTM)	An employer, employee, student, and participant working at distance (also known as remote, collaboration) to submit a work project for a virtual team
Virtual Team Skills Assessment	A test administered to virtual team members to evaluate their skill sets and perspectives regarding working at a distance

Overview of the Virtual Team Global Business Model

As explained above, the Virtual Team Global Business Model is applicable to anyone working at a distance on collaborative projects. Both business professionals and students can use the model as a guide to working collaboratively with others. The model begins with goals, objectives, and tasks that are designed by management. Preceding the goals, objectives, and tasks are deliverables communicated by project managers or team leaders to employees/participants working remotely. The deliverables are then executed within the framework of virtual team guides by employees working collaboratively on projects, known as the virtual team members (VTMs). In each category, there are communication strategies and accountability. In essence, the fluidity of the project begins with management clearly defining goals, objectives, and tasks.

Figure 1.1 shows the full Virtual Team Global Business Model. Each element will be discussed with examples in the subsequent chapters.

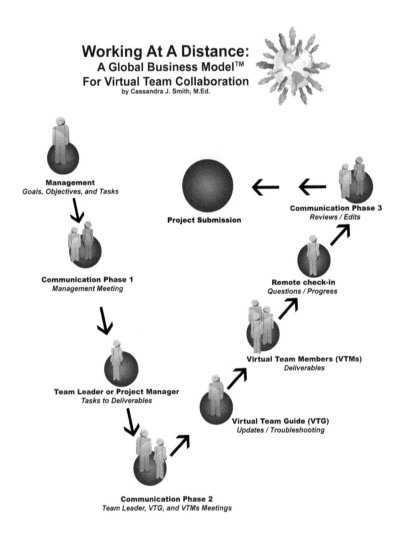

Figure 1.1   Virtual Team Global Business Model™

CHAPTER 1: REVIEW

The *Virtual Team Global Business Model* provides a structure for employees working at a distance. The model is based on a *people-driven philosophy*. People have to communicate *synchronously* at a number of points when working at a distance in order to complete tasks effectively. Having a model to follow, and logical action steps within the model, promotes fluid communication and enables performance gaps to be closed, keeping remote workers connected. The VTML provides employers, employees, and participants who are functioning collaboratively with a hierarchical working process, precise steps to follow, a lucid communication flow, process standards that relate to specific tasks, and clear expectations about *deliverables*.

Management play a key role in the VTML, setting up the foundation for the project. Management may consist of one person or a team of managers involved in the distance project. Depending on the scope of the project, the numbers of management members who help to create virtual teams may vary, but whatever the case, management must have a strong presence in virtual teams and designing the goals, objectives, and tasks for remote workers using the VTML.

Team leaders and *project managers* are the next categories of individuals involved in ensuring the success of virtual teams. Using the VTML, team leaders and project managers are responsible for designing deliverables from tasks defined by upper management so that the virtual team guide and virtual team members can create and execute the deliverables.

Virtual team guides and *virtual team members* are responsible for producing the deliverables. Both groups will communicate, along with management, throughout the duration of the project to bring the distance project to fruition.

The underlying principle in using the VTML for distance work is *clear communication*, leading to top-level collaborative project performance.

MANAGEMENT USING THE VIRTUAL
TEAM GLOBAL BUSINESS MODEL

INTRODUCTION: MANAGEMENT ROLES

Management

In Chapter 1, I stated: "In essence, the fluidity of the project begins with management clearly defining goals, objectives, and tasks." When these three elements are defined and cogent, the pathway is set for management's expectations of employees to bring the project into fruition. Management should be responsible for defining goals, objectives, and tasks for the entire virtual team project. This assignment could include a management team or an individual, depending on the scope of the project. Clear sets of expectations in the form of goals, objectives, and tasks lead to clear communication, cadence, and greater fluidity for members working at a distance, collaboratively, in virtual teams.

Defining goals, objectives, and tasks is easier said than done. Sometimes these groups of information begin to read like a list of commands as opposed to capturing the data needed by employees. If management understand the scope of the virtual team and its members, this helps to define each of these groups of information. In a professional survey on virtual teams, one of the participants commented: "Understanding how to effectively manage a virtual team will be beneficial both academically and professionally. There is an increase in tele-commuting in many offices and depending on the job, you may work virtually with people across the country on various projects." Management have to consider the interaction among these groups and understand the culture. Chapter 5 will discuss these topics in more detail, along with how to manage diverse teams. For now, let's consider how goals, objectives, and tasks should be devised.

GOALS

Goals are often statements that explain the desired outcomes for a project and provide insight into ideal and precise results. Goals should clearly articulate to employees and all members working at a distance what should be accomplished in a short sentence. Goal setting is an essential part of management's duties. Even when management assume that goals are understood by employees, data reports or assessments of the project may reveal a different picture. As a manager, you may be left wondering what happened and why data reports reveal discrepancies in your virtual team collaboration project advancement. For example, you manage six virtual team groups. You meet with your teams using Webconferencing. You have a PowerPoint presentation that displays the course of actions and where your teams are heading. You log off the meeting and breathe a sigh of relief, confident that your virtual team groups are good to go and work on the project. Are you noticing how the performance gap is increasing between what you think the employees understand and what they actually understand? There have to be process standards in place, elements where employees can communicate that they understand, as well as evaluation components. Keep reading, and you will fully understand how it all works!

A viable goal includes verbs to describe the desired outcome such as *increase, reproduce, manufacture,* and *complete.* Goals are specific to the needs of the company. A good way to devise goals is to ask questions such as: "What do I envision occurring in my endeavor, project, quest?" "How will I obtain results?" "What variables will need to be in place?" Goals are outcome-driven, and demonstrate the bottom line of the project.

Consider the following scenario that will be used throughout this book to illustrate how the VTML operates for businesses and virtual team employees.

O-SPAN YOUTH'S E-COMMERCE PROJECT

O-Span Youth, a manufacturer of children's shoes, is expanding its operations into e-commerce. This is a major project that will have several components involving its companies in North America, Latin America, and Europe. The North America location is where the corporate office is located, and will be responsible for operating the e-commerce system once it has been developed. But Mr. Wilcox, CEO and Manager of Operations, has locations in other regions assisting with the e-commerce project development. Wilcox, along with feedback from stakeholders, has provided the following goals for this new endeavor:

1. Increase sales by offering the buying and selling of children's shoe products online.
2. Compose an Internet marketing plan for e-commerce.
3. Form business-to-business electronic markets.
4. Develop an e-customer service team.

5. The goals for this project are action-oriented, and demonstrate the desired end results. By offering e-commerce to customers, Wilcox and the stakeholders are hoping to increase sales, compose a marketing plan that is e-commerce-driven, form partnerships with other e-markets, and develop a customer service team for e-commerce purchases. The goals for this project have been set in place.

OBJECTIVES

Objectives support goals; they are often results derived from specific goals. In a training scenario, objectives explain what trainees will know how to accomplish once the training is completed. Working at a distance, objectives should consist of a preview of the responsibilities to be completed. In essence, the objectives should mirror the goals for the project. Management should set objectives based on the project needs.

Objectives are the project needs that should be met—elements of the action step-based goals to help form the project. Objectives should also be specific. Objectives should include verbs similar to goals and action-oriented steps that provide a quick overview of what the employee should have accomplished by the end of the goal. Notice in the O-Span Youth example that the objectives define specific teams that will work on the project and which objectives should be met by those teams.

O-Span Youth's Objectives for its E-commerce Project

Goal 1: Increase sales by offering the buying and selling of children's shoe products online.
Objective 1: Virtual teams in Latin America and Europe design database.
Objective 2: Virtual teams in Latin America and Europe integrate products.
Objective 3: Virtual teams in Latin America and Europe create an online transaction order process.

Goal 2: Compose an Internet marketing plan for e-commerce.
Objective 1: Virtual teams in North America define marketing tools.
Objective 2: Virtual teams in North America create an online advertising campaign.
Goal 3: Form business-to-business electronic markets.
Objective 1: Virtual teams in North America, Europe, and Latin America develop e-partnerships.
Objective 2: Virtual teams in Europe create specialty products for business solutions.
Goal 4: Develop an e-customer service team.
Objective 1: Virtual teams in Latin America and Europe set up customer service support.
Objective 2: Virtual teams in Latin America and Europe set up phone support for Internet consumers.
Objective 3: Virtual teams in Latin America and Europe create automated data collection functionality for consumer profiles.

Objectives can be designed as management desires and according to what fits logically for the project. Depending on the scope of the project, there may be several goals, several objectives, and several virtual teams. The O-Span Youth example demonstrates how collaboration among the same-country virtual teams and global virtual teams will work on the projects. Virtual teams for your company may be set up for distance work depending on the skills of your employees and the infrastructure of your company. In essence, some managers may find it useful to follow the VTML objectives when they have to manage several virtual teams in different countries, while others may use the VTML for virtual teams within the same country. Either way, the VTML can be effective in enhancing communication and defining clear expectations for virtual team workers.

TASKS

Tasks are specific steps derived from the objectives that need to be completed. Tasks are the processes the virtual teams will complete. If the goals and objectives take the form of action steps, then the tasks will not be as challenging to define following the same design. Management are still active in this phase of the Virtual Team Global Business Model. Management define the tasks after they have defined the goals and objectives. If objectives are a preview of responsibilities, then tasks are specific responsibilities that are categorized under each objective. Tasks are action-oriented in nature, and demonstrate the precise roles employees will fulfill in each department or virtual team location. How would management make tasks work with the technology available? A simple way to accomplish this is to be well organized, to communicate, and to coordinate the work. Creating tasks is not a rush job! There should be a systematic order to composing tasks for each objective, and this may require management to communicate with several other managers, subject matter experts, and supervisors in order to solicit the help needed to define tasks.

Continuing the O-Span Youth example, review the following tasks under the objectives.

> Goal 1: Increase sales by offering the buying and selling of children's shoe products online.
> Objective 1: Virtual teams in Latin America and Europe design database.
> Task 1: Meet for data specifications and planning.
> Task 2: Create database layout and interface.
> Task 3: Develop database security systems.
> Task 4: Add beta-testing data for quality checks/database performance.
> Objective 2: Virtual teams in Latin America and Europe integrate products.
> Task 1: Populate content (pictures/text) in database.
> Task 2: Select pricing and add to database.
> Task 3: Create content for specialty advertisements.

Objective 3: Virtual teams in Latin America and Europe
create an online transaction order process.
Task 1: Develop an interface for e-checkout.
Task 2: Secure the e-checkout process.
Task 3: Test the e-checkout process.

As the manager of operations, if your project calls for four goals and you need four objectives and four tasks, there is a good deal of uniformity. However, if you do not need as many objectives or tasks to meet the goals, that is also fine. The number of categories does not impact the VTML as long as you meticulously capture the elements needed to complete the project for your remote workers.

Wilcox Composes Goals, Objectives and Tasks

Mr. Wilcox has composed his goals for O-Span Youth's e-commerce project. He solicits help from stakeholders and his management team to flesh out the objectives and tasks for his staff.

After considerable amounts of time allocated to the primary steps for this project, management are confident that they have established and finalized goals, objectives, and tasks for the e-commerce project.

MANAGEMENT'S TIMELINE EXPECTATIONS AT A DISTANCE

Recall the introduction, where management might not have conveyed the goals and objectives clearly, and ambiguity around expectations could result in delays for employees working at a distance. In the O-Span Youth example, the manager has defined his goals, objectives, and tasks.

The final element from management in the model should include a timeline. Management should define when they expect the product to be completed, keeping in mind the necessity for any drafts, testing, and iterations that might be required. When designing timelines, management also should keep in mind that some parts of the project are subsequent parts of the main design. Therefore, the main design has to be completed before the other parts can be accomplished. If the project needs to be completed by May 2014, after management has finalized the goals, objectives, and tasks, monthly reports from employees might be ideal. Such a monthly timeline might be effective or not, once again depending on the scope of the project.

Table 2.1 shows an example of a timeline for O-Span Youth's e-commerce project.

Table 2.1   O-Span Youth's timeline

O-Span Youth e-commerce project	Deliverable due dates 2013–14	Project points
Management Goals Objectives Tasks	March 31	During March, management will finalize goals, objectives, and tasks for the e-commerce project and set deadlines
Communication Phase 1 Management meeting	April 15	Management has a synchronous meeting with Project Manager Daniels
Team Leader Tasks to deliverables	June 25	Daniels completes steps to prepare deliverables and administers a Virtual Team Skills Assessment to the VTMs by the due date
Communication Phase 2 Deliverables review	July 31	Daniels, VTG Roberts and the VTMs have a synchronous meeting to start the deliverables (project results) process by the due date
VTG/VTMs Work in progress	August 15– December 15	Roberts and the VTMs begin working on the deliverables

Remote Check-in Q&A session	September 20–October 20 November 15	Roberts meets with the VTMs for troubleshooting and to provide updates on the deliverables to Daniels
Communication **Phase 3** Edits/iterations	February 25	Roberts reports to Daniels, and any drafts, edits, or updates are implemented
Project submission	May 2014	

These dates from management, along with the defined goals, objectives, and tasks, should be communicated to the next group of participants in the VTML, the team leaders or project managers; this is called Communication Phase 1.

Communication Phase 1

Communication Phase 1 consists of a meeting to explain the scope of the project, involving senior management and the leaders who will be responsible for conveying the information to the VTMs. Communication Phase 1 entails management meeting with the team leader or project manager to preview the goals, objectives, tasks, and timelines for project deliverables. This is an important step in the VTML collaboration process. If management omit this step, if management do not communicate audibly, if no sign of the communication process (clear instructions, active listening, decoding the message) is transferred, the team leader may make assumptions about this major project, perhaps based on an email or some other type of correspondence. The project will then be object-driven, not people-driven. In essence, Communication Phase 1 should include a synchronous meeting of some sort where management communicates the goals, objectives, tasks, and timelines. This synchronous meeting should allow for one or more question and answer sessions so that the team leader or project manager understands what deliverables to convey to the virtual team guide (the facilitator of the virtual team) and VTMs.

Note: At all points in the communication phases, it is important for management to check in and obtain updates from the team leaders or project managers.

During Communication Phase 1, management can present goals, objectives, tasks, timelines and/or ideas on a Virtual Team Project Form. The project form should highlight important information about the project and preview some of the major areas. This form can be reviewed during Communication Phase 1 meeting in a PowerPoint presentation using synchronous software such as Adobe Connect. Here's an example of a Virtual Team Project Form for O-Span Youth:

Virtual Team Project Form

O-Span Youth's E-commerce Project

Mission: To make comfortable and safe shoe products for children and distribute them worldwide.

Goals:

1. Increase sales by offering the buying and selling of shoe products online.
2. Compose an Internet marketing plan for e-commerce.
3. Form business-to-business electronic markets.
4. Develop an e-customer service team.

Virtual Teams: North America, Latin America, and Europe

Objectives and Tasks: *To be distributed to each team leader.*

Comments: *Teams will work in assigned departments to complete the e-commerce project by May 2014.*

The Virtual Team Project Form provides an overview of the project. Management can then distribute the goals, objectives, and tasks on a separate form to the leaders of each virtual team, especially if the forms are going to several departments and virtual teams.

Here's another example:

Virtual Team Project Form

Database Design Team

Objective 1: *Virtual teams in Latin America and Europe design database.*

Tasks:

1. *Meet for data specifications and planning.*
2. *Create database layout and interface.*
3. *Develop database security systems.*
4. *Add beta-testing data for quality checks/ database performance.*

The team leader will then add deliverables (discussed in Chapter 3) to the Virtual Team Project Form before distributing it to team members. This might seem like a lot of work, but once management have identified the tasks under the objectives, it is then a matter of the team leader or project manager inserting the defined deliverables and disseminating a form to each virtual team group responsible for those deliverables.

E-COMMUNICATION FLOW

As you review the practical yet powerful use of the VTML, it is important to remember that the main purpose of the VTML is to provide a process flow for good communication throughout the project so that employees or students working at a distance can understand and feel secure in the knowledge that there is accountability and help at each stage of the project development.

Since management's roles have now been established, this is a good juncture to emphasize and reiterate the communication flow before proceeding to Chapter 3's discussion of deliverables.

More traditional communication models involve someone sending a message, and the receiver decoding the message then providing feedback. There is scope for error in interpreting the message because of the influence of nonverbal clues and perceptions. Now, with advances in technology and more opportunities to communicate, the potential communication gap due to nonverbal cues, perceptions, and the misinterpretation of messages has increased.

Review the following e-communication flow process:

Message → Technology → Metamessages →
Acknowledgement → Interpretation

Most conflicts and issues when working face-to-face or remotely result from communication issues. A message is formulated and sent, but the sender is unsure whether the receiver has understood it. In face-to-face communication, listening may not occur if the receiver is preoccupied with deciding on a response, forming thoughts about what was delivered in the message, or has unresolved issues with the sender. Online, these issues also apply, in addition to the challenge of distance. Another point about traditional forms of communication is that a lot of emphasis is placed on the sender's message not being perceived with the original intent. However, virtual messages with technology components emphasize the sender's intent, distance lines of communication, and the receiver's interpretation.

As a manager, keep in mind that when you are developing your goals, tasks, objectives, and timelines, you are using technology to deliver at a distance, and you are still engaging with humans. This shows how important the communication process still is today in keeping misinterpreted messages to a minimum. Exhibiting the first part of the communication model is easy: the sender of a message. As people, we send messages often. However, with the use of technology such as email, asynchronous forms of communication, and social media, the middle to end part of the communication model tends to be neglected, leaving the sender wondering whether the primary aspect of the model—the message—has been understood.

HOW DOES E-COMMUNICATION FLOW RELATE TO THE VTML?

A review of the communication flow model is pertinent to the VTML because technology is involved in working at a distance. Technology and electronic metamessages are now a large part of the communication model because online conversations can be one-sided and inaccurate. Being mindful of a people-driven (VTML) philosophy when working with technology in business means that management need to ensure that there are opportunities for voice-to-voice communication, as explained in the VTML. Metamessages are often nonverbal interpretations of a message that can be likened to the noise that traditional communication models included, such as thoughts or feelings about the issue that often lead communicators to perceive a message incorrectly. Using the VTML, clear instruction is provided for each group involved in the virtual team project, and opportunities for active listening and participation are incorporated so that messages are decoded correctly.

Let's take a closer look at e-communication flow as it relates to working at a distance.

Message → Technology → Metamessages →
Acknowledgement → Interpretation

Message

A message might consist of an email from one VTM to another, or a document from the VTG or team leader. A deliverable can be a message to another VTM. In the VTML, messages are usually a written form of correspondence, but can also include synchronous voice exchanges— and these are always beneficial when communicating at a distance. Messages may come from a vast range of sources when working online, including any member of a virtual team, such as the manager, team leader or project manager, subject matter experts, VTGs, or VTMs.

Technology

Technology includes the software and hardware components involved in working at a distance: the computer, keyboard, distance education software, and any asynchronous communication tools used to originate and receive and reply to a message. Technology also includes the lines of communication, which can sometimes lead to a lot of lag time, for instance if a message is not delivered, or is delivered late. When thinking about this new e-communication flow, a good rule of practice is to think about all the issues that have occurred with technology when trying to communicate, and the implications of those issues for response styles and decision making styles. If workers at a distance, no matter what their role, bear these factors in mind, then reacting to delays, communication challenges, and working with colleagues may improve.

Metamessages

Metamessages are the nonverbal assumptions made about a message. As stated above, metamessages may be accurate or inaccurate. They derive from unknown factors about the message, perceptions, emotions, established or unestablished relationships between sender and receiver. Sometimes limited knowledge about technology can originate a metamessage. Metamessages can occur between any group, sender or receiver, leader or employee when working at a distance. The tone of email is an example of metamessaging. If individuals think about the term "email tone," this does not originate in the email message itself. What are resonating are inner thoughts, metamessages, perceptions about the message.

Acknowledgment

Acknowledgment is a separate item from interpretation in our consideration of e-communication flow because when using electronic communication, an acknowledgement can be sent in the form of an email, but that does not necessarily mean that the receiver has understood the message. If the message is not something the receiver wants to receive or read, acknowledgement can be emotional—composed in haste and based on an inaccurate representation of the original message.

Interpretation

Interpretation, known more traditionally as feedback for some types of communication, includes how a message is decoded and processed. In online interactions, messages that elicit feedback that accurately reflects the intent of the receiver result in accurate deliverables, or perhaps new insights into the deliverables and expectations for the remote project may enhance the original message, as often results when working with diverse groups to improve product quality. Interpretation can be problematic when working at a distance because of all of the factors mentioned above in the absence of voice-to-voice communication.

The main point is that e-communication flow is people-driven; there needs to be voice-to-voice communication to reduce the influence of metamessages, inaccurate interpretations, and confusing messaging back and forth. E-communication flow is one reason why VTML check-in points for deliverables are important.

Consider the following scenario using a technology-driven communication flow that is not people-driven (no voice components).

Message

> To: Davis (Team Leader)
> Cc: Eaton, Reynolds, Bibbs
>
> Hello Team,
> I have created my e-advertisement list, and I am concerned that I have not received feedback from Christos. I have sent several emails, and I do not want my list to be repetitive. We are on the same team, so I need a review before sending to the other virtual team members in North America to place in their Marketing Tool package. Can you all help?
>
> Collins

Technology

Email engagement.

Metamessage

Christos feels as if Collins is saying that he is not pulling his weight on the team and is ignoring his message—as noted in the acknowledgment below. There are several messages that could be conveyed, not only from Christos's and Collins's perspectives, but from that of everyone copied into this email, including Davis, to whom the email is addressed. Metamessages from the group might include perceptions such as lack of organization, poor leadership, a slacker on the team, and concerns about how other North American team members may view their team.

Acknowledgment

Christos responds:

"I have been inundated with emails from everyone that you copied in on this message. I have sent you feedback. What are you referring to in this message? Are you kidding me? The list is on file. I don't appreciate you calling me out in front of everyone like I am a slacker on the team."

Interpretation

Collins responds:

"Christos, I am trying to get the project completed and had not heard from you. I was not trying to be rude. I do not have any messages from you. In fact, I am wondering how you can respond to this message and not my others."

Davis responds:

"Christos, I do not think Collins was 'calling' you out. I think that she might have made a mistake. I received your feedback and have forwarded it to her. I pulled it from the team e-room. That is where we were supposed to have submitted it, Christos. I hope this helps."

A simple misunderstanding as to where a deliverable should be located can lead to confusion in teams working at a distance, let alone copying several persons in on an email. The ensuing interpretations and dialogue are potentially limitless without any resolution. It is important to check all areas where team members work in case emails are accidentally going to the spam folder or the message/feedback is in another location where the team members work.

One point about communicating using technology is that emails need to be specific and then followed up by voice contact to help avoid miscommunication and the need for numerous responses. Voice contact and synchronous meetings are vital when working at a distance.

CHAPTER 2: REVIEW

Management are responsible for starting the project flawlessly to help remote workers understand expectations. Management must be clear about what they want and must consult subject matter experts, if needed, so that expectations of the project for all involved are seamless. The initial stages that involve management's responsibilities include defining goals, objectives, tasks, and timelines, following the VTML.

Goals are desired outcomes that are action-oriented, providing a preview of project expectations. Goals should explain in a short sentence what is expected and what the final project result should be for remote workers. *Objectives* support goals and preview the responsibilities of employees to complete the goals. Objectives often include specific teams that will accomplish precise tasks. Tasks are steps that will demonstrate that the goals are in progress. *Tasks* include the job that needs to be completed and hands-on work that must be submitted to show that progressive steps are being made by remote workers to achieve the goals.

Management must communicate with team leaders or project managers in Communication Phase 1, explaining the goals, objectives, tasks, and timelines for the project. This meeting should take place in a synchronous format to enable clear communication and guidance. The e-communication flow allows cogent communication among participants, employees, or students working at a distance. Understanding that, while technology is a huge component of working at a distance, people are the driving force of that technology provides control over the process and avoids metamessages that may be inaccurate when working collaboratively.

MR. WILCOX PRESENTS IDEAS

Mr. Wilcox and management are ready to present the project to Jim Daniels, the Project Manager. The Communication Phase 1 meeting is scheduled next week.

Wilcox presents the ideas for O-Span Youth's e-commerce project to each department using the Virtual Team Project Form.

TEAM LEADERS OR PROJECT MANAGERS USING THE VIRTUAL TEAM GLOBAL BUSINESS MODEL

INTRODUCING THE TEAM LEADER OR PROJECT MANAGER ROLES IN THE VTML

**Team Leader
or
Project Leader**

Chapter 2 pointed out that the team leaders or project managers need to understand what deliverables to convey to the virtual team guides and virtual team members. In essence, this is the reason for Communication Phase 1. Whether in higher education or business projects, there has to be a team leader or a project manager to oversee the progress of the team and project. These serve as a point of contact for VTMs before upper management review the deliverables. Following the VTML, creating and reviewing deliverables are the main responsibilities of the team leader or project manager.

Communication Phase 1

In Communication Phase 1, together with upper management, the team leader or project manager defines the goals, objectives, tasks, and timelines for the project, either verbally or electronically from any handouts or the Virtual Team Project Form. The team leader or project manager will also gather any additional information needed, and prepare to communicate their tasks to the VTGs and VTMs. However, before doing this, the team leader or project manager must perform several important steps, the most important of which consists of developing a list of deliverables.

What are Deliverables?

Deliverables are tangible or intangible (for instance, electronic) items such as templates, databases, product samples, video or audio files, training guides, text documents, assignments, or any other items that signify that progress is being made towards goals and project completion. Deliverables are the evidence that the goals, objectives, and tasks have been met.

Converting Tasks into Deliverables

The first step involves the team leader or project manager converting the tasks into deliverables. It's a good idea for the team leader or project manager who is composing the list of deliverables to be a subject matter expert and knowledgeable about diverse departmental functions, since he or she will be responsible for overseeing and presenting the deliverables from VTMs to management. The team leader or project manager also needs to confirm to upper management that deliverables are of the required quality. The team leader or project manager therefore bears a lot of responsibility when converting tasks into deliverables. This job has to be accomplished accurately and to fully represent the specifics required by the project design. If your team leader or project manager is not a subject matter expert, then he or she may have to refer management's recommendations to a subject matter expert, or alternatively include in the team two or three personnel from the technical, business development, and creative departments who are experts. In essence, the team leader or project matter ensures that the deliverables are being accomplished, are being accomplished accurately, and are of sufficient quality to submit to management. If there are several team leaders or project managers, you should hold joint meetings, since they are responsible for transforming the tasks into deliverables for their remote workers (VTMs). The VTML can be followed regardless of the number of staff appointed to each role.

Note: Another role a team leader or project manager might take on is appointing a virtual team guide if management are not assuming this role. The team leader or project manager oversees the development of deliverables for the remote project, while the VTG works directly with the VTMs, keeping track of progress, issues, and providing updates to the team leader or project manager. Chapter 4 will discuss VTGs in greater detail.

Bear in mind that the tasks management define are converted into deliverables by the team leader or project manager. Some tasks identified by management are not as complex to convert into a deliverable.

Using the O-Span Youth example, let's review how a team leader or project manager might convert tasks into deliverables. Notice that each task represents the associated deliverable: for example, Task 1— deliverables for Task 1, Task 2—deliverables for Task 2, and so on.

> Goal 1: Increase sales by offering the buying and selling of children's shoe products online.
> Objective 1: Virtual teams in Latin America and Europe design database.
> Task 1: Meet for data specification and planning.
> Deliverables for Task 1:
> Compose lists of ideas.
> Plan to discuss any foreseeable challenges and resolutions.

The simple deliverables for Task 1 include composing a list of ideas about the project to initiate discussion about it. Other deliverables are more complex. For example:

Task 2: Create database layout, interface.
Deliverables for Task 2:
Set up interfaces.
Create database.
Task 3: Develop database security systems.
Deliverables for Task 3:
Run security check.
Produce security report.
Task 4: Add beta-testing data for quality checks/database performance.
Deliverables for Task 4:
Simulate testing processes.
Produce evaluation report.

Database design and planning are required to avoid issues arising later. The team leader or project manager must be knowledgeable about specific elements of the design, or otherwise solicit the assistance required to prevent issues and major project delays arising in future. For any distance project, The specifications must be as precise as possible so that the conversion of tasks into deliverables represents specific processes. Let's review some more examples of the conversion of tasks into deliverables using the O-Span Youth project.

Objective 2: Virtual Teams in Latin America and Europe integrate products.
Task 1: Populate content (pictures and text) in database.
Deliverables for Task 1:
Review graphics in stock.
Collect new graphics.
Create text captions.
Task 2: Select pricing and add pictures to database.
Deliverables for Task 2:
Design price lists for first roll-out of 100 shoe products online.

Task 3: Create content for specialty advertisements
Deliverables for Task 3:
Identify first specialty roll-out products.
Set up advertisements for specialty selections.

In the examples above, the tasks were all related to Goal 1 and the first two objectives that were transferred into deliverables. Now, let's try converting the tasks into deliverables for Goal 2.

Goal 2: Compose Internet marketing plan for e-commerce.
Objective 1: Virtual teams within North America define
    marketing tools.
Task 1: Select marketing tools.
Deliverable 1: Compile social media, blogs, email, and
    television contacts.
Task 2: Create marketing directory.
Deliverable 2: Develop directory listing for marketing brands.
Objective 2: Virtual teams in North America create online
    advertising campaign.
Task 1: Create e-marketing plan.
Deliverable 1: Develop cost analysis and media
    e-advertisement material.
Task 2: Draft e-marking plan.
Deliverable 2: E-design marketing sketch.

Each task has to be converted into a deliverable, so this is a detailed undertaking for the team leader or project manager. Each task should have one or more deliverables that are as specific as possible to help VTMs understand the expectations of them.

Task 2 for the Goal 1 deliverable for O-Span Youth consists of drawing up a template for the e-commerce database design. Converting a task into a deliverable requires the team leader to assess what is needed to complete that deliverable. To reiterate, if the project manager or team leader is not fully aware of the steps needed to perform tasks, it is advisable to enlist the help of a subject matter expert. The subject matter expert can chronicle the specifics needed for a task, thereby helping the team leader or project manager to create the deliverables for the VTMs. Here are some examples of other deliverables that might be required for different projects:

- marketing plans
- scripts
- delineation of job functions
- standard operating procedures
- cost sheets
- computer programs
- data models.

Timelines

The next task is to draw up timelines for the deliverables. These timelines are different from management's in Communication Phase 1, but management's timeline can serve as an example. It is prudent for the team leader or project manager to work within management's monthly time frames or adopt the timeline specified by management. If the project is due to be completed by May 2014, for each month during the interim period the VTG/VTMs should be set deliverables to submit to the team leader or project manager for finalization before the deadline allocated by management. If the manager has set a deadline of delivering a draft by October 2013, a good working virtual team under the guidance of a VTG would have drafts approved by the team leader and ready to submit by September or perhaps even August 2013. Sometimes deadlines will not be realistic, depending on the scope of the project, but progress toward the end result is what matters. Progress assessment allows the team leader and management to see whether timelines need to be adjusted more realistically once production begins and the project needs are being met.

Along with the timelines, team leaders or project managers should give an estimate of how many hours it should take the remote workers to complete the deliverables. If the remote workers need to allocate 30–40 or 40–50 hours a week, the level of expectations should be considered and documented. Members may spend more or less time depending on their work ethic and their dexterity in accomplishing the tasks, but the VTMs need to know the expected timelines for deliverables. This is important when employees are working at a distance, since an estimate of the work hours required will them to manage their time and adjust their schedules in terms of what they need to accomplish each day given their other life responsibilities. Management should be realistic, understanding that virtual team workers have other life events that are occurring. Throughout this book we will discuss some best practices for management to help VTMs to communicate with their peers.

Skills Assessment

The next task the team leader or project manager should complete before allowing the VTMs to embark fully on the project is to assess their strengths and weaknesses. If employees are working in different countries and there is an IT department in Europe and an IT department in Latin America, which one will complete the database design—and complete it effectively—and/or will both work on specific parts of the project, as in the O-Span Youth project? Conducting a Virtual Team Skills Assessment of employees in the group and establishing their specialties will assist in this decision. Such an assessment helps management to enlist the best talent among geographically dispersed individuals to complete the project. If this assessment is submitted to management early enough, it may inform the decision about which teams will work on which parts of a project, especially if management need assistance—this is another area that is contingent on the specific organization and the scope of the project. The assessment can also allow employees working at a distance to supplement other members' skills, and if necessary, can help the team leader, project manager, or VTG to organize subgroups of remote workers to complete certain deliverables. Here is an example of a Virtual Team Skills Assessment form.

VIRTUAL TEAM SKILLS ASSESSMENT

General Teamwork

1. Identify your strengths when working with others in teams at a distance.
2. Identify your weaknesses when working with others in teams at a distance.
3. How would you rate the following in order of importance:
   a. participation?
   b. managing conflict?
   c. team member skill development?

Roles within Distance Teams

4. When working in a virtual team, how would you classify your likely role out of the following:
   * **I'll do it**—assume responsibility when no other team member volunteers or is active?
   * **passive**—likely to participate only after everyone else engages?
   * **assertive**—take the lead and tell others what to do?
   * **slacker**—avoid working to advance the team project?

5. When working at a distance, do you prefer to:
   * organize?
   * direct?
   * participate?
   * observe?

Skills Assessment

6. Classify your skills, then be specific about the tasks you can do in each of these categories (for example, if you have strong writing skills, describe your writing strengths, such as writing advertisement text, academic writing, writing copy material, writing blogs, or editing):
   * writing
   * designing
   * developing
   * leading
   * organizing
   * other skills.

7. List the software programs you feel comfortable using to communicate or work with virtual teams (for example, email, Skype, social media, Microsoft programs, graphics programs).

8. List the software programs you feel you need training in to enhance your skills (for example, email, Skype, social media, Microsoft programs, graphics programs).

Communication at a Distance

9. Working at a distance, which aspect of the tasks do you find most problematic:
   a. communicating with coworkers/peers?
   b. understanding task and expectations?
   c. other (describe)?
10. In teams, do you tend to meet or beat deadlines?
11. How do you resolve conflict (for example, compromise, accommodate, ignore, suggest)?
12. Describe the types of virtual team workers you feel most comfortable working with on projects (for example, problem solvers, immediate responders, procrastinators).
13. Describe your decision making process.
14. How often do you like to check in with your other virtual team members?

Perceptions at a Distance

15. Do you see projects as a whole, or chunk them into manageable tasks? Provide a practical example of your response.
16. Do you like concepts, ideas, and theories? If so, how does this affect your work in groups at a distance?
17. Do you like facts, details, and specific information? If so, how does this affect your work in groups at a distance?
18. Describe your initial perception of working at a distance.
19. Rate how you think you perform on virtual teams regarding the quality of your work (exceptional, good, fair, poor).
20. Rate how you think you are likely to participate consistently (extremely high participation, good participation, average participation, poor participation).

This assessment form includes several open-ended questions so that the VTG can evaluate the employees' responses and determine their preferred working styles when collaborating on projects at a distance. There are no numerical data behind the assessment, but instead a commonsense approach to how team members can work to their strengths. Formal personality, learning style, and decision making assessment tests have been evaluated, but some managers don't use any of them. This example of an assessment form is meant to serve as a guide if no data are available to clearly categorize participants. The Virtual Team Skills Assessment highlights areas that allow management to determine which employees will be most effective as remote workers.

The "General Teamwork" section asks participants to identify their strengths and weaknesses. Team leaders or project managers assessing the results can align team members accordingly, based on their skills. For example, if members of the database design team all have the same skills, it may make sense to keep the team members together, and subgroups may not be needed. Subgroups are smaller groups within the team that will help with the development and deliverables in more focused areas. Team leaders or project managers may find subgroups helpful, based on the assessment results. If within the database design group there happen to be members with strong technical skills and strong troubleshooting skills, it may be best to set up two subgroups within the database design team: a technical group and a troubleshooting group.

Another important area to emphasize in general teamwork is that team members need to have the skills or training needed for their tasks. Therefore, team skill development is high on the list of priorities. The skills involved could range from understanding how to work in teams to understanding how to navigate technology to improve work performance. Once the required skills are in place, members are likely to feel more comfortable and more likely to participate, especially if they clear about performance expectations. Conflict management is important, and is an ongoing activity. Once teams have been established, skills have been assessed, and members are participating, any conflict that occurs should be more manageable, because the majority of conflict ensues when members feel they are taking on an unfair share of the work or are ill-prepared to work at a distance, and especially to do so in collaboration with others.

The "Roles within Distance Teams" section of the assessment can be problematic if not managed properly. If a few employees are doing the majority of the work, conflict often ensues. The "I'll do it," "passive," "assertive," and "slacker" roles are common in higher education virtual teams. Some students may fail to complete their parts of assignments, but if instructors do not check in regularly, those students may obtain the same grade as the team members who have been more active, leading to resentment. (The VTML as it relates to higher education is discussed in detail in Chapter 6). The VTML allows for this by ensuring more accountability for the roles that emerge. Some employees won't admit during the assessment that they are slackers, but they may admit that they don't like working at a distance or that they prefer to observe. The main point with the roles is to be aware of them as a manager and to encourage members to participate, or to explain the policies, procedures, and expectations to employees who may be causing conflict by exhibiting behaviors that are counterproductive for the team.

Skills assessments are an effective indicator of where the strongest team members should be placed and whether any subgroups are needed. Employees' skill sets can be wide-ranging and beneficial for team development. A skills assessment allows the team leader or project manager to evaluate the strengths of VTMs, but using open-ended questions rather than providing a range of options allows employees to evaluate their own skills, potentially providing greater insight. This emphasizes that employees have options and that they can work where they feel best suited, not where management feel they fit best, as long as they have answered the questions truthfully and management take the time to review and assess the results properly. It is a good idea to seek open feedback from employees by including a comments section in the assessment form. This provides employees with an opportunity to discuss where and on which types of projects they would prefer to work in the virtual team. Providing these options improves communication because employees can express their desires, enhancing employee morale and providing management with documentation of what the employee stated when the virtual team project gets under way.

Technical skills in working online are extremely valuable. Employees have to communicate through asynchronous forms of communication such as email, newsgroups, distance education software such as eCollege as well as synchronous meetings and conferences, so all participants need to be familiar with Web-based meeting programs such as Adobe Connect, Elluminate Live!, or Cisco WebEx that allow for group collaboration. Management often assume that employees using such collaboration tools are proficient in them, but this is not always the case. A technical skill assessment is important so that management can supply any training required. Identifying and improving employees' diverse and advanced technical skills are important to ensure the success of virtual teams.

As we've established, communicating at a distance can be challenge, and the VTML can help to bridge any communication gaps. The assessment allows issues about how members working at a distance can stay in contact to be addressed through the active presence of the VTG and team leader or project manager. This consistent interaction helps employees to communicate with their coworkers in virtual teams. The assessment also enables employees to understand that some members may easily work to deadline, while others may need additional explanations of deliverables and expectations.

The main benefit of having VTMs engage in this series of questions stems from understanding how team members communicate and how they may respond to conflict. Ensuring availability and having back-up plans when people are not available are good strategies when trying to work at a distance. The "Communication at a Distance" section can also be helpful for managers. For example, if the team leader understands that a group of individuals works to deadline, allowing padding time in the schedule before deliverables have to be submitted to management may be a good idea. This section of the skills assessment can also reveal different approaches to resolving and making decisions about conflicts. Conflict management will be discussed in more detail in Chapter 4.

The "Perceptions at a Distance" section is a good conversation-starter during Communication Phase 2 (discussed below), allowing the team leader or project manager to invite members to comment on how they view working at a distance, and their concerns about it. Many such concerns can be resolved through discussions, and the fact that the VTML ensures that there is a lot of accountability and support will help to clarify some perceptions about working at a distance. During these discussions, the VTML can be explained in more detail, and members can share their thoughts about the assessment questions. Encouraging employees to discuss how they perceive and resolve issues and how these actions influence team dynamics can generate rapport with other members they will be working with at a distance. These discussions can also provide employees with an opportunity to assess their likeliness to participate and perform, and whether their performance is likely to be of high quality or substandard. These types of discussions can be conducted during a chat session or even an initial remote check-in, as discussed in Chapter 4.

The Virtual Team Skills Assessment adds value to team assignments and helps remote workers to understanding their colleagues. The assessment can be supplemented with questions about personality, decision making, motivation, and learning style, depending on your organization and the dynamics of your employees. Good managers will devote time to assessing these areas and understand that people have different learning styles, resolve issues differently, and have diverse work ethics that influence distance work. A well-designed skills assessment can produce information about your employees that might otherwise never be discovered. Assessments are also great ways to encourage discussions among VTMs, building trust among the teammates. The topics of trust and team building will be discussed in more detail throughout the book.

Wilcox and Daniels' Meeting and Deliverable Conversion

At the end of Communication Phase 1, Mr. Wilcox provides Project Manager Daniels with the goals and objectives for each department. Daniels starts work on converting the tasks to deliverables.

Goal 1: Increase sales by offering the buying and selling of children's shoe products online.

Objective 1: Virtual teams in Latin America and Europe design database.

Task 1: Meet for data specification and planning.

Deliverables Task 1: Compose lists of ideas, plan to discuss any foreseeable challenges and resolutions.

Task 2: Create database layout and interface.

Deliverables Task 2: Set up interface and database template.

Task 3: Develop database security systems.

Deliverables Task 3: Run security check, produce security report.

Task 4: Add beta-testing data for quality checks/database performance.

Deliverables Task 4: Simulate testing processes, produce evaluation report.

Objective 2: Virtual Teams in Latin America and Europe integrate products.

Task 1: Populate content (pictures/text) in database.

Deliverables Task 1: review graphics in stock, collect new pictures, create text captions.

Task 2: Select pricing and add in database.

Deliverables Task 2: Design pricing lists for first roll out of 100 shoe products online.

Task 3: Create content for specialty advertisements.

Deliverables Task 3: Identify first specialty roll-out products, setup advertisement for specialty selections.

(Objective 3) Virtual Teams within Latin America and Europe creates online transaction order process.

Task 1: Develop interface for e-checkout.

Deliverables Task 1: Create e-checkout databases.

Task 2: Secure e-checkout process.

Deliverables Task 2: Setup database security.

Task 3: Test e-checkout process.

Deliverables Task 3: beta-test process and submit report.

Goal 2: Compose Internet marketing plan for e-commerce.

(Objective 1) Virtual teams within North America defines marketing tools.

Task 1: Select marketing tools.
Deliverables 1: Compose social media, blogs, email and
television media list/plan.
Task 2: Create marketing directory.
Deliverables 2: Develop directory listing for marketing brands.
(Objective 2) Virtual teams within North America creates
online advertising campaign.
Task 1: Create e-marketing plan.
Deliverables 1: Develop cost analysis, media
e-advertisement material.
Task 2: Draft e-marking plan.
Deliverables 2: e-design marketing sketch.
Goal 3: Form business to business electronic markets.
(Objective 1) Virtual teams within North America, Europe,
and Latin America develop e-partnerships.
Tasks 1: Develop e-partnerships.
Deliverables 1: Setup e-business proposal, Create
e-business list, contact prospective e-partnerships.
Tasks 2: Provide e-partnerships information to Information
Technology.
Deliverables 2: Submit e-partnerships information to IT for
populating in database.
(Objective 2) Virtual teams within Europe create specialty
products for business solutions.
Tasks 1: Identify specialty products.
Deliverables 1: Meet with Marketing and submit ideas for
specialty products.
Tasks 2: Develop advertising content.
Deliverables 2: Create text for advertising content, Gather
pictures for specialty content.
Tasks 3: Submit to Information Technology.
Deliverables 3: Categorize items, submit pricing lists.
Goal 4: Develop e-customer service team.
(Objective 1) Virtual teams within Latin America and Europe
setup customer service support.
Tasks 1: Create databases for customer service area.
Deliverables 1: Submit customer service template.

Tasks 2: Test customer service area.

Deliverables 2: Beta test customer service support, run reports and analyze results.

(Objective 2) Virtual teams within Latin America and Europe setup phone support for Internet consumers.

Tasks 1: Compile phone support.

Deliverables 1: Provide numbers for phone support, test, provide reports.

Tasks 2: Train employees on phone support.

Deliverables 2: Create training manuals, hire employees, setup employee training dates.

(Objective 3) Virtual teams within Latin America and Europe create automated data collection functionality for consumer profile.

Tasks 1: Create AIDC database.

Deliverables 1: Submit template for customer profile and object identifiers.

Tasks 2: Test system.

Deliverables 2: Run automation and submit reports.

Daniels reviews deliverables and is ready for Communication Phase 2.

 **Communication Phase 2**

COMMUNICATION PHASE 2

Now that the team leader or project manager has converted tasks into deliverables and assessed virtual team members' skills, it is time for Communication Phase 2.

Communication Phase 2 consists of the team leader or project manager meeting with the virtual team guide(s) and virtual team members via synchronous communication to review the deliverables. At this point, the VTMs have completed no actions to progress the project other than completing the skills assessment. The team leader or project manager should establish clear deliverables so that VTGs and VTMs understand the expectations and due dates.

During Communication Phase 2, the team leader or project manager explains the Virtual Team Project Form, as was done with management during Communication Phase 1. At this point, the Virtual Team Project Form should be updated to include deliverable information. Following the meeting, the VTG should distribute copies of the form to each department, identifying the specific deliverables expected for each group. Communication Phase 2 should also include time for questions, so that the VTG and VTMs are clear about expectations before leaving the meeting. As with Communication Phase 1, this meeting must be synchronous with audio and chat components, so that employees can communicate their initial concerns and questions.

Here is O-Span Youth's Virtual Team Project Form. Notice that team members are made aware of the peers who will help them complete deliverables because this information is noted on the forms.

Europe Virtual Team Project Form

O-Span Youth's E-commerce Project

Mission: To make comfortable and safe shoe products for children and distribute them worldwide.

Goals:

1. Increase sales by offering the buying and selling of shoe products online.
2. Compose an Internet marketing plan for e-commerce.
3. Form business-to-business electronic markets.

4. Develop an e-customer service team.

Deliverables: Teammates Latin American Office

Compose list of ideas.
Plan to discuss foreseeable challenges and resolutions.
Set up interfaces and database template.
Run security check.
Produce security report.
Simulate testing process.

Latin America Virtual Team Project Form

O-Span Youth's E-commerce Project

> **Mission:** To make comfortable and safe shoe products for children and distribute them worldwide.
>
> **Goals:**
>
> 1. Increase sales by offering the buying and selling of shoe products online.
> 2. Compose an Internet marketing plan for e-commerce.
> 3. Form business-to-business electronic markets.
> 4. Develop an e-customer service team.
>
> **Deliverables: Teammates European Office**
>
> Create e-checkout database.
> Beta-test process.
> Submit evaluation report.
> Set up e-proposal.

North America Virtual Team Project Form

O-Span Youth's E-commerce Project

Mission: To make comfortable and safe shoe products for children and distribute them worldwide.

Goals:

1. Increase sales by offering the buying and selling of shoe products online.
2. Compose an Internet marketing plan for e-commerce.
3. Form business-to-business electronic markets.
4. Develop an e-customer service team.

Deliverables: Teammates North American, Latin American, and European Offices

Contact e-market partners.
Create e-design marketing template.

The Virtual Team Project Form should list all the deliverables the team is responsible for completing. In addition to the Virtual Team Project Form, it may be beneficial to make a deliverable diagram that includes all of the deliverables for each department available in a location where all team members have access. The diagram can be designed by the team leader or project manager, and should provide a review of how all the deliverables work together and a pictorial representation of each expected deliverable so that VTMs can review it while working on their specific deliverables. This diagram can be drawn up using software such as the Mapping program to produce an attractive visual, or could take the form of an Excel chart that clearly demonstrates the deliverables flow.

SYNERGY AND VIRTUAL TEAMS

At the point where Communication Phase 2 is implemented, leaders or supervisors are now in direct contact with other leaders (VTGs) and employees (VTMs). The constant and consistent interaction among management and groups working remotely promotes synergy when working in virtual teams. Synergy is another major factor in the VTML, where it is defined as:

> *a community of virtual team members working in harmony with consistent interaction and engagement with support from strong, present leadership.*

Strong, present leadership helps to overcome communication problems because communication channels are more uniform when leaders engage actively, ensuring that all remote workers have access to the same shared information. Employees must be familiar with the types of communication they will use to work at a distance and where to locate information shared by the leadership.

In essence, synergy within virtual teams begins with the leadership. Maysa Hawwash, Director of Talent Management Solutions at Drake International in Toronto, has commented that a leader's job is to understand the roles and personality traits of virtual team members. The more leaders understand about their employees when working in teams, the easier it is to work to team member's skills and strengths. In this way, with diverse teams, synergy can be enhanced.

Maysa Hawwash has observed that there are four types of teams:

1. **functional team**—permanent in nature—its goal does not change over time;
2. **cross-functional team**—assembled of people from multiple departments and focused on a project with a specific timeline;
3. **self-directed team**—operates without direct management;
4. **virtual team**—works from afar toward a common goal, communicating through the Web or by phone.[1]

---

1   Maysa Hawwash, "Building Synergy in Teams," DrakePulse, May 1, 2013, www.drakepulse.com/2013/05/building-synergy-in-teams/ (accessed December 17, 2013).

What is consistent regarding the different types of teams is that synergy can be created when leaders ensure that teams understand their purposes, can work autonomously on their parts of projects, and are enabled to work interdependently to meet team goals. Another point about virtual teams is that at any given point, the virtual team can encompass all types of teams. Virtual teams can be functional and permanent in nature. Some of the literature treats virtual teams as temporary, but if a company develops products using remote workers or has the need for services at a distance, virtual teams can be long-term. Technology and the use of e-commerce have resulted in more distance working. Virtual teams can be cross-functional while being geographically dispersed and having specific timelines for completion before moving on to the next deliverable or project. Virtual teams can be self-directed in the sense that at some points, VTMs have to complete tasks autonomously to then interact with team members and offer their submissions, garner feedback, and make edits. Virtual teams have a common goal. Virtual team members work using Web-based technologies to communicate and submit deliverables. They also work by phone and via asynchronous or synchronous communication channels.

Synergy can be a concern when working in groups at a distance because the substance of a team depends on its members working in that team. If everyone is participating and knows what is expected, the team flows well. However, the chances are that this is not the reality among many teams. Some team members may not participate, trusting their peers to complete the work. Given direct contact with leaders and the guided help that the VTML advocates, synergy is improved for remote workers, enhancing trust within virtual teams.

Susan Wright-Boucher is a Canadian Recruitment and Staffing Industry Professional specializing in recruitment strategies, employer branding, online marketing, employment trends, and social media. She says: "A virtual team must build the same sense of community and shared purpose."[2] The key is that VTMs must understand that purpose.

---

2   Susan Wright-Boucher, "Virtual Teams: Creating Synergy," Plugged In Recruiter, August 29, 2011, http://swrightboucher.wordpress.com/2011/08/29/virtual-teams/ (accessed December 17, 2013).

In the VTML, purpose is defined by management in the form of goals, objectives, and tasks.

In the same article, Wright-Boucher advocates that ideally, teams should:

> *Take time to build trust with team members one-on-one before you begin virtual team meetings. Members of a virtual team who know they are trusted will be more forthcoming with ideas and will challenge group thinking in a healthy way. Use one-on-one time to ensure each team member understands the bigger picture and is aligned with the individual contribution they can make.*[3]

The Communication Phases and Virtual Teams Skills Assessment are occasions for building team camaraderie and trust using the VTML.

TRUST AND TEAM BUILDING

Other team building activities that will help remote workers to establish relationships with teammates at a distance include establishing team events. Team activities are not meant to distract employees from their jobs, but to foster teams working across different regions and remotely. VTMs can have a weekly "Check-in Friday," when they share ideas on any topic that is not necessarily work-related (although including that aspect is a good strategy), but focuses instead on fun discussions about their families, culture, activities shared with friends such as cooking or building, customs, traditions, and so on. "Expertise Hours" can be another useful activity, when employees share their how-to skills: How to install a new sink? How to design a basic Web page? How to write a blog? How to resolve conflict?

There are numerous ways to get virtual teams involved and establish rapport among their members. These employees will work with one another, so team building is necessary to let them familiarize themselves with each another. Holding a team activity once a month

---

3   Ibid.

or every two months is a good idea. This could be accomplished via another synchronous meeting using Adobe Connect that is open to all members. You could make a few meetings mandatory, especially during start-up. Other activities can be optional. If needed, the roster that is kept of participation in these meetings can indicate the extent to which members have been active. If there are certain groups who consistently do not participate, offering incentives may help to improve team participation. These activities might seem counterproductive, but distance work needs attention. It is easy to meet with others face-to-face, but online, developing creativity and connection resonates, and promotes shared trust and participation.

CHAPTER 3: REVIEW

In *Communication Phase 1*, the team leader or project manager is responsible for drawing up *deliverables* from tasks that management has composed. In order to establish deliverables, tasks need to be converted into items that will need to be completed. Deliverables often serve as evidence that the goals, objectives, and tasks have been met. Deliverables can be simple or complex, depending on the project's needs. Team leaders or project managers should also create *a timeline* for deliverables to serve as a guide for virtual team members. The team leader or project manager can also appoint *virtual team guides* to help virtual team members to complete tasks at this stage of the VTML.

Team leaders or project managers also administer the *Virtual Team Assessment Form* to virtual team members. This is an evaluation of skills and communication strategies used to help identify any potential areas of communication barriers, the roles of virtual team members working at a distance that are often displayed, and perceptions of working with groups at a distance that members often have that may or may not be true. Evaluating the results of the assessment can help team leaders or project managers to understand their team dynamics and facilitate more effectively.

Communication Phase 2 places team leaders or project managers in direct contact with virtual team guides and virtual team members to communicate the deliverables. The communication phases can contribute to synergy within virtual teams. Management leadership is important with regard to synergy. Management set the pace for virtual team members to work together, building trust among teams working at a distance. When teams are synergized, employees are likely to work effectively because they know that their colleagues understand their contributions and challenges.

COMMUNICATION PHASE 2: DANIELS AND ROBERTS

Project Manager Daniels selects Ms. Liv Roberts as his VTG for the e-commerce project. Daniels holds a meeting with Roberts and the VTMs using Adobe Connect. He explains the deliverables using the Virtual Team Project Form, then sends Roberts the forms listing the deliverables for each department so that the VTMs can begin work.

VIRTUAL TEAM GUIDES AND VIRTUAL TEAM MEMBERS
USING THE VIRTUAL TEAM GLOBAL BUSINESS MODEL

VIRTUAL TEAM GUIDES

Virtual Team Guide (VTG)

In Chapter 3, I stated, "The team leader or project manager should establish clear deliverables so that VTGs and VTMs understand the expectations and due dates." In Communication Phase 2, team leaders or project managers have communicated the project plan, project needs, and deliverables to the VTMs and VTGs, so those two groups are responsible for deliverables at this point. The VTGs are responsible for keeping the team leader abreast of any issues and the fluidity of the project, meeting with any other VTGs of virtual teams located elsewhere for updates, making sure that the team is flowing and that the VTMs have any assistance required to complete the project deliverables, and ensuring that all submissions are gathered into one packet or one area in the company's software, such as e-room, where the team leader and management can check progress on deliverables. The VTGs' main role is facilitation, helping to keep the virtual teams moving fluidly and managing deliverables. The VTML focuses on accountability: each member of the group is accountable, and if one of them is not contributing to completing a task, then management can assess the situation appropriately by targeting roles that are not being fulfilled.

The VTGs might be individuals from each satellite location—in our O-Span Youth example, Europe, North America, and Latin America—who meet, troubleshoot, and assess progress to help team members to work cohesively. Naturally, if VTGs are managing several groups, they play a huge role in managing the deliverables and deciding on the specific responsibilities each VTM will work on to complete them. Since the team leader or project manager has administered the Virtual Team Project Form, all VTMs are in the loop about the expected deliverables, and VTGs can ensure that they are allocated correctly and fairly. Drawing on the O-Span Youth example, consider the following distribution of deliverables.

North America has eight employees working on a virtual team that will be responsible for defining the marketing tools. The deliverables include social media contacts, blogs, and television media. Each member could be assigned multiple tasks to bring the deliverables to completion. This could be based on their skill sets, experience, and the overall group makeup identified by the VTG based on input from the team leader or project manager. The VTG can list each VTM's name on an Excel spreadsheet to keep track of which member is responsible for each specific deliverable. Although employees working in virtual teams may do more than what is listed for them, the general idea under the main deliverable provides some guidance. Also, bear in mind that VTMs will usually know what they have to complete based on what they were hired to do and the information on the Virtual Team Project Form. For example, the marketing team VTMs understand that they are responsible for developing a marketing plan, and they understand how to bring this to fruition because they have been informed through the VTML.

Table 4.1 shows an example of how VTGs can manage deliverables.

Table 4.1 **Virtual team guide spreadsheet**

Team Member 1	Bibbs	Blog	Completed
Team Member 2	Bouse	Social media	In progress
Team Member 3	Collins	Social media	Completed
Team Member 4	Christos	Television	In progress
Team Member 5	Davis	Blog	In progress
Team Member 6	Eaton	Blog	In progress
Team Member 7	Earls	Television	In progress
Team Member 8	Reynolds	Television	In progress

Based on the skills of VTMs, each of them has a specific task to complete individually and collaboratively as they work to complete the deliverables. VTGs should also be skilled in communication strategies for businesses and working remotely, including having a proven active presence working online and effective conflict management skills. VTGs take on a conflict resolution role to ensure that teams are working together to submit their deliverables. For example, if O-Span Youth Marketing Team member Rogerus in Latin America is working with O-Span Youth Marketing Team member Baccus in Europe, the VTGs must ensure that both are active, and not waiting for one or more other team members to complete their own tasks. A successful VTG implements weekly check-ins with virtual team groups. These can consist of telephone calls, emails, and assistance with deliverables. A review of VTMs' work should also be part of the active VTG presence. A Virtual Team Progress Form should be implemented halfway through the project, setting out the progress of each VTM. Here's an example of a Virtual Team Progress Form.

VIRTUAL TEAM PROGRESS FORM

Employee name: _____

Deliverable(s): _____

Rate deliverable(s):

Excellent   Good   Work in progress

Comments on rating: _____

_____

Virtual Team Presence Status Indicator:

A—active

S—steady

N—needs work

Comments on Presence Indicator: _____

_____

The Virtual Team Progress Form is not meant to grade VTMs, but to make them aware of where they need to improve and how important their deliverables are when working at a distance. It allows for a quick assessment of deliverables and provides VTGs and team leaders or project managers with a document to review as well as the opportunity to suggest any feedback for improvement. With regard to the Virtual Team Presence Indicator on the Virtual Team Progress Form, "active" means that the VTM is responding to emails and has a strong presence in his or her team; deliverables are being submitted on time, and the work is of sufficient quality. "Steady" means that the VTM has a good team flow, but could be more active and follow through more with his or her colleagues. It may also mean that the VTM's deliverables are satisfactory. The "needs work" indicator means that the VTM has significant lag time in responding to his or her colleagues and is falling below expectations for the project.

In order for VTGs to make an accurate assessment of VTMs' work and evaluate them using the Virtual Team Progress Form, the VTGs themselves must be active . They must respond to emails, have access to the software required to review the deliverables VTMs are working on, and be able to review the dialogue between VTMs. There has to be a central location for communication, especially for the major parts of the project. Quick answers to VTMs can be conveyed by emails, but when it comes to deliverables, testing of deliverables, and drafts, all should be in view of the VTGs and team leaders or project managers. An inclusive area is required to establish an accurate portrayal of teamwork at a distance.

For any member participating in the VTML, it is also a good idea to have proxies so that if one VTM is unavailable, the proxy is already familiar with the team leaders, the VTGs' roles, and VTMs' progress so that he or she can step in and complete or oversee tasks seamlessly. It's a good business strategy to keep a log of processes and progress so that a proxy can take over the job of any VTM who is unavailable or affected by unexpected events.

CONFLICT MANAGEMENT PROTOCOL FOR THE VIRTUAL TEAM GLOBAL BUSINESS MODEL

As explained above, VTGs have to have diverse communication skills, including those involved in conflict management. They must ensure that there is a conflict management protocol in place for VTMs. They do not have to undertake this role alone. Management may already have a conflict protocol in place. If not, it is a good idea to establish a systematic procedure for conflict resolution so that VTMs feel comfortable and reassured that they will have access to support when needed. According to research by Joseph Grenny, co-author of the *New York Times* best-seller *Crucial Conversations*, when people face challenges with a colleague who works in a different location, they may resort to silence or other passive coping strategies, or they may become verbally violent or attacking toward their colleague.[1] These verbal attacks can spiral out of control, leaving teams and team members silent and inactive. This impacts the overall production of the project and employee morale. Remember that the VTML is established on a people-driven philosophy. If VTMs are unhappy, confused, and isolated in their feelings when working at a distance, the project will suffer, so it is helpful to engage VTMs who are willing to resolve issues through communication and for management to ensure that an effective conflict protocol resolution process has been established.

Virtual team guides can implement the following processes for conflict resolution.

Have VTMs Try to Resolve the Issue Themselves

In the initial stages, VTGs can encourage VTMs to resolve any conflicts that may arise. The VTMs will need to decide whether they have a genuine issue that needs to be resolved, or whether it perhaps results from a personal agenda and their desire to conduct tasks in their own way. If the issue is pressing and it appears that it needs to be addressed respectfully, VTMs should contact each other, preferably using the telephone or Skype, to establish a clear understanding of the issue. It is always a good idea to keep a record of the dialogue to establish a paper trail of the conflict resolution process.

Have Employees Contact the VTG

If VTMs can't overcome an issue themselves, VTGs should encourage the VTMs to enlist their help to try to resolve the conflict. This is another occasion when some type of verbal discussion is needed, because emails can be impersonal and are prone to misinterpretation. One option is to set up a meeting between the parties to discuss the issues, reflect on the progress on deliverables, and try to get to the

---

1   Kerry Patterson, Joseph Grenny, Ron McMillan, and Al Switzler (2012), *Crucial Conversations: Tools for Talking When Stakes are High*, 2nd edn., New York: McGraw-Hill.

bottom of the problem, or as a last resort in cases of extreme conflict, reassign some of the VTMs.

Have VTMs Contact the Team Leader or Project Manager

Before contacting the team leader or project manager, VTMs should contact their VTG. If the VTG can't resolve the issue or if it involves the VTG, then the team leader or project manager will need to be brought in to bridge the conflict gap. If the VTG has to reassign a VTM, he or she should inform the team leader or project manager. Ideally, conflict should be resolved by the VTMs themselves, unless it has to do with the process flow or product development and is impeding progress.

To manage conflict, VTGs can ensure the following:

- Check in regularly during the work day with all the teams you are responsible for guiding.
- Intervene, don't ignore—send messages and call meetings if the conflict between VTMs is unmanageable.
- Ensure that process standards are followed (process standards are reviewed in Chapter 5).
- Review the deliverables, and compliment good work and good efforts—this boosts employee morale and affirms that high-quality work is being noticed.
- Keep teams on track—don't let members get distracted by pettiness.
- Reinforce team goals so that deliverables are a priority—sending monthly reminder emails and messages using the virtual team software or work calendar helps to keep timelines in mind.
- Have a Plan B—this could involve a proxy or skilled workers who can cross-train in different areas to help to ensure that deliverables are submitted on time.
- Keep a current spreadsheet showing who is doing what—a tracking method aids organization when managing multiple individuals or projects.

Virtual Team Members (VTMs)

VIRTUAL TEAM MEMBERS

The next and final important group for detailed consideration in the VTML is the virtual team members themselves. VTMs are the employees working at a distance who will do the majority of the development work for projects. VTMs are responsible for completing the deliverables to bring the project to completion. At this point, VTMs are aware of the project and the deliverables as a result of Communication Phase 2. They are ready to work on their deliverables and get started under the guidance of their VTG. Each team member is responsible for one or more deliverables or collaborating with another team members to complete them. The timelines are set in place, and the team leader or project manager knows who is responsible for which part of the assignment.

VTMs are the heart of the company. The virtual team group collaboration allows VTMs to build on each other's skills. They are the employees who will submit the deliverables, work with their cohorts at a distance, be assessed on their deliverables, and in essence try to work effectively at a distance. The VTML provides some relief and ameliorates several communication barriers and concerns about working at a distance due to its hierarchal structure, strong focus on communication, and the accountability it provides.

CRITICAL THINKING AND ADULT WORK ETHICS

At this point, the VTMs are ready to work in their assigned groups with guidance from their VTGs, and they are clear about their deliverables. However, when they are engaging with their coworkers, it helps them to work effectively and avoid getting distracted by individuals' different work ethics if they are aware of three important best practices, each of which requires an element of critical thinking.

Critical thinking is a thought process that involves assessing and analyzing a situation, and possibly assessing the thought patterns behind a decision or the implementation of an action. Critical thinking as it relates to working with others at a distance involves understanding situations from others' perspectives, such as their work ethics and learning styles, not reacting emotionally to correspondence or comments, managing conflict more effectively, and being aware that allocating time for working at a distance is a necessity.

Best Practice 1: Be Aware that Virtual Team Members Will Work in Their Own Ways to Accomplish Their Tasks

VTMs can reduce a lot of anxiety when working at a distance if they understand individuals' different work ethics, learning styles, and response styles to situations.

Some pride themselves on overachieving, submitting high-quality work, and have issues when others in teams submit substandard work. Some members work to deadline, while others work ahead of deadline. Some prefer to work close to a deadline or respond to peers as their schedules permit within reasonable project timescales. Some members are satisfied with meeting the requirements of a task—no more, no less.

Work ethics
Differences in work ethics are inevitable because people are not the same and will not approach tasks the same way when working face-to-face, let alone when working at a distance. VTMs need to be aware

of this. As with any argument about ethics, what is considered a poor work ethic by one person might be considered a good work ethic by another. Procrastination is an example of this subjectivity about the work ethic. Some people work well to deadline, while others prefer to work as soon as instructions have been provided and they understand expectations.

Learning styles
There are several ways to process information. The most common are visual, auditory, and tactile learning. Sending pictures to another VTM in the form of complicated graphics may be fine for some employees, while others may need accompanying text and explanations. It is prudent for VTMs to understand the diversity of learning styles, and when engaging with their peers and coworkers, to consider additional steps such as note-taking, diagramming and offering examples when communicating and trying to explain processes or when providing instructional guidance.

Response times
Individual response times must be considered when working with others. Some VTMs may assume that a reasonable timescale for a response when working at a distance is within the same day, while others may think it reasonable to respond within 24 hours. Some VTMs may be take longer, depending on their schedules—although it is a good idea to check in regularly and respond immediately with an acknowledgement, even if it will take more time to provide the response required. However, it is helpful for management to define reasonable response times, taking into consideration the lag time involved when working at a distance.

If conflicting work ethics are leading to problems and deliverable targets are not being met, this should be addressed, as explained in the discussion of the conflict protocol. However, if VTMs are not responding as quickly as the specific needs of other VTMs dictate, but nevertheless within a reasonable timescale, it is important to understand that this may reflect an individual work ethic, rather than necessarily meaning that the member is failing to meet expectations.

These personal variations will be discussed in more detail in the section "Virtual Team Members—the Heart of the Organization" below.

Best Practice 2: Apply Critical Thinking to Resolve Conflicts

When managing conflict, VTMs should be reminded of the perceptions of working at a distance they may have identified and discussed when completing the Virtual Team Assessment Form. Every instruction and constructive critique should not be interpreted as derogatory. E-communication flow is a good example of how feelings of isolation when using technology and perceiving metamessages can influence emotional reactions online. VTMs should remain logical as opposed to emotional, and be able to distinguish between the two, asking themselves questions such as: "Are my feelings because these remarks are hurtful, or does this team member have a point?" or "What am I despondent about regarding this scenario?" This sort of emotional assessment should be undertaken before responding to a conflict situation. The most practical way to confront conflict is to address the problem in a non-threatening manner without hostility.

Grenny's research shows that $1,500 and an eight-hour workday are gained for every conflict avoided in the workplace. He advises organizations interested in curbing the costs of conflict to teach their employees how to speak up quickly and effectively when they have concerns with their colleagues. He offers four tips to get started:

1. **Confront the right problem**—The biggest mistake people make is to confront the most painful or immediate issue and not the one that gets them the results they really need. Before speaking up, stop and ask yourself, "What do I really want here? What problem do I want to resolve?"
2. **Rein in emotions**—We often tell ourselves a story about others' real intent. These stories determine our emotional response. Master communicators manage their emotions by examining, questioning, and rewriting their story before speaking.
3. **Master the first 30 seconds**—Most people do everything wrong in the first "hazardous half-minute"—like diving into the content

and attacking the other person. Instead, show you care about the other person and his or her interests to disarm defensiveness and open up dialogue.

4. **Reveal natural consequences**—The best way to get someone's attention is to change their perspective. In a safe and non-threatening manner, give them a complete view of the consequences their behavior is creating.[2]

Best Practice 3: Apply Critical thinking to Time Management

Time can be a key factor for anyone working on a project at a distance because the demands of the rest of their life, with all its responsibilities, compete for their attention. It is necessary to consider how time is being spent and whether VTMs are wasting time that could be allocated to work or other responsibilities. A time management calendar can provide an overview of how much time is being taken up by specific tasks. Although no time management tool is perfect, this can offer a helpful visual assessment of how one's time is being spent. If working from home, it can be easy to become distracted by other responsibilities like managing the household. Time must be allocated to the virtual team. Since VTMs are the heart of the project, they must stay in contact with their colleagues as they work to submit deliverables. If there are pressing personal issues that will take a VTM away from the team project, the VTG should be informed so that proxies can step in and take over the work. Table 4.2 shows an example of a time management calendar.

Applying critical thinking to time management not only helps VTMs to organize their own time, but as with learning styles and response times, it brings recognition that their coworkers at a distance have their own life events and responsibilities as well. This can encourage VTMs to be proactive rather than reactive in their emotional responses when working with others, realizing that they are coping with the rest of their lives,

---

2   Press release, "Cost of Conflict: Why Silence is Killing Your Bottom Line," VitalSmarts, April 6, 2010, www.vitalsmarts.com/press/2010/04/cost-of-conflict-why-silence-is-killing-your-bottom-line/ (accessed December 17, 2013).

Table 4.2 Time management calendar

Time	Monday	Tuesday	Wednesday	Thursday	Friday	Saturday	Sunday
6 a.m.	Send/check emails	Send/check emails	Send/check emails	Send/check emails	Send/check emails	Send/check emails	Send/check emails
7 a.m.	Log in to virtual team software to work—check for updates/ messages from VTMs and VTG	Log in to virtual team software to work—check for updates/ messages from VTMs and VTG	Log in to virtual team software to work—check for updates/ messages from VTMs and VTG	Log in to virtual team software to work—check for updates/ messages from VTMs and VTG	Log in to virtual team software to work—check for updates/ messages from VTMs and VTG	Log in to virtual team software to work—check for updates/ messages from VTMs and VTG	Off
8 a.m.	Work on Deliverable 1	Work on Deliverable 1	Remote check-in	Discuss issue #1 with team members	Work on Deliverable 1	Off	Off
9 a.m.	Work on Deliverable 1	Work on Deliverable 1	Off	Work on Deliverable 1	Work on Deliverable 2	Work on Deliverable 2	Work on Deliverable 2
10 a.m.	Remote check-in	Q&A session with VTMs	Check in with VTMs on resolution for issues	Make edits	Work on Deliverable 2	Off	Off
11 a.m.	Send/check emails	Send/check emails	Send/check emails	Remote check-in	Send/check emails	Send/check emails	Send/check emails

Table 4.2   Time management calendar *continued*

Time	Monday	Tuesday	Wednesday	Thursday	Friday	Saturday	Sunday
12 noon	Lunch	Lunch	Finalize Deliverable 1	Submit Deliverable 1 draft	Work on Deliverable 2	Off	Off
1 p.m.	Work on Deliverable 2	Meet with team members	Lunch	Lunch	Lunch	Off	Off
2 p.m.	Work on Deliverable 2	Submit draft to VTG	Edits	Edits/in progress Team Latin America needs to review	Remote check-in	Lunch	Off

some VTMs may be unavailable on certain days or at certain times of day, and time has to be allocated for work and communication in among all these variables.

Notice that at this stage in the VTML, there is less responsibility on VTMs to decipher what deliverables should be completed because this has already been clearly defined. At this point, the VTMs are responsible for working together to submit their deliverables. Virtual collaboration is streamlined because the VTMs have a clear idea of what they should be doing, as opposed to guessing, figuring out who they should be working with, and spending significant amounts of time trying to contact other team members while still taking care of their other everyday obligations.

VIRTUAL TEAM MEMBERS—THE HEART OF THE ORGANIZATION

The VTML ensures that management are involved and sets the tone of the project with goals, objectives, and tasks. Team leaders or project managers are aware of deliverable needs because they have done the work to create the deliverables based on tasks. Team leaders or project managers are in a position to help VTGs to oversee the progress of deliverables and assess VTMs' progress. There is accountability throughout the model. VTMs have every virtual base covered, and are ready to engage with their colleagues. All that is left is for the VTMs to get to work!

As the title of this section indicates, virtual team members are the heart of the organization with regard to working on remote projects. They are the employees, groups, and participants who can either bring the project to fulfillment with high-quality results, or falter, ending the project with low-quality or even no results. Attention must be devoted to how VTMs will communicate among themselves. The VTML provides a guide for how to ensure this, and if all participants follow it, it ensures that help and support are available when necessary. However, the VTMs still have to do the work. They are unlikely to contact their VTG or team leader or project manager about every quandary or conflict presented in their teams. Adults tend not to work that way, and will engage as they know best or have learned to over time. Adults have their own ways of knowing and doing, as we have addressed above. VTMs, the heart of the organization, must understand how to engage and what is considered acceptable engagement when working with others. When adults understand, they are empowered to adjust or adapt to ways of knowing or learned behaviors as required.

What Does Engagement Between VTMs Look Like?

In the VTML, Communication Phase 2 included making VTMs aware of their deliverables and imparting information to them via the Virtual Team Project Form. This brings them to the point where they are ready to begin their work. Assuming that the VTMs have been trained in the technology they will use to engage with their coworkers (which will be dealt with in more detail later when discussing best practices for using technology with virtual teams), the following steps illustrate with examples how to begin to complete the deliverables and engage with coworkers.

Completing Deliverables

Now that VTMs know what is expected, they can start work on completing their deliverables. Details of these have been sent to them via email using the Virtual Team Project Form and communicated verbally in the Communication Phase 2 meeting. Each VTM knows what his or her team is responsible for doing and completing.

For example, one of the deliverables in the O-Span Youth project is to populate content in the database. The database has to be designed by the Latin America and Europe design teams. Therefore, the VTMs working on populating the content within these groups may not begin work until the database is completed. They may be able to gather preliminaries and undertake tasks that will have the content drafted and close to submission, but full teamwork may not begin until the database system is framed. That is fine. Team members still should check in regularly and participate.

When they check in, they should engage via the virtual team company software provided—a vital component for virtual team interaction. Using this, they should be able to leave a trail of messages in threads and then have a separate area within the program to submit the parts of the deliverable they are working on and/or have completed. They must be clear about where to submit the deliverable, so a specific area within the virtual team company software system should be allocated and each VTM must understand that this is where all their deliverables should be submitted. Depending on the project, the VTG may still have to gather them into one submission to present to upper management, but there should be a central location for all deliverables.

This is when applying critical thinking to time management, as explained above, is significant for each VTM. Each day, the VTM will allocate time to work on the project. The timeline must include time to design the larger pieces of the project. There should be clear expectations of how many hours should be allocated to the project, at least per week, so that progress can be made. Drawing up person-hour estimates is the responsibility of the team leader or project manager, as explained in Chapter 3. Employees will have deadlines and expected time to complete the work defined by management, so the schedule VTMs create for themselves should include time for any projects contingent on someone else in the team. If VTM are using time management calendars or designing their own calendar of tasks, these should realistically reflect their own progress, schedules, and the interaction with other team members required to complete deliverables and take care of other responsibilities. They should set out a scheduled routine of what they are waiting on for completion, what they plan to accomplish within a particular hour, and whatever else is expected. Adhering to such routines ensures consistency and emphasizes that the virtual team project must take priority and participation is essential.

Garnering Feedback from VTMs

The hours allocated to work consist of VTMs working on the deliverables and garnering feedback from other team members. This is the heart of true virtual team engagement. When couples become engaged, this signifies a pending commitment. The same applies to virtual teams. When VTMs engage with other members consistently, this signifies a commitment to the team. True virtual team engagement occurs when VTMs realize that their part of the project matters. However, they may depend on another VTM to complete it. Garnering feedback from VTMs is an essential aspect of working at a distance— true virtual team engagement. The sooner the deliverables from each VTM are completed, the sooner feedback from other VTMs can be received. Working individually to complete tasks is inevitable when working at a distance, but a major aspect involves submitting that individual deliverable to the team to create a whole part—a whole deliverable (the original intent of management stated in the initial goals). VTMs need to constantly bear in mind that each portion, each contribution, each part of the deliverable contributes in the whole (solidifying true virtual team engagement) as they consistently garner feedback from one another.

Let's review an example of the importance of garnering feedback.

O-Span Youth's Latin America and Europe teams are responsible for creating an online transaction order process for the e-commerce project. This task requires several of O-Span's companies and several servers. VTMs from each group are gathering input for the system and ensuring that the computer platforms of each company can handle customers' orders. Five VTMs on the Latin America virtual team and four team members on the Europe virtual team are responsible for input gathering. Next, seven team members are engaged in testing input in Europe to ensure that customers' orders can be dealt with. The input gatherers from both teams have to complete their deliverables before testing can begin.

Testers can move forward with evaluation once input has been gathered.

This example illustrates how important gathering feedback and engagement are for team members working at a distance. Conventional teams work together on projects and are accountable to each other. The same should apply when working at distance—true virtual team engagement.

VTMs to VTMs Check-in

Garnering feedback is important but so is responding to emails and instant messages. These tools should be utilized because they often signify active engagement. The company's extranet should be updated so that VTMs, VTGs, team leaders or project managers are kept up to date about any company developments that will influence project development for virtual teams. It's helpful to incorporate a tracking system of some sort to determine how many times remote workers check in to the virtual team company software system where they submit deliverables. Some software packages can track participation as well as numbers of clicks on certain objects. If management make checking in with the team a priority, VTMs will in turn make it a priority to deliver high-quality projects and do their jobs well. If VTMs are working actively, they should receive support and credit for this.

Checking in regularly should also consist of providing feedback about other VTMs' deliverables—another aspect of true virtual team engagement. Providing constructive comments and sharing knowledge can help each part fit into the whole. This needs to be a two-way process. Providing feedback on deliverables is as much part of true virtual team engagement as receiving feedback.

Expressing Opinions and Decision Making

VTMs should not be afraid of expressing opinions and making decisions when engaging in feedback or pointing out issues to their teammates. The mindset that "I'm staying in my own lane" is not prudent when working with others on virtual teams. One of the consistent values of virtual teams is the diverse perspectives they embody. Embracing such diversity can lead to excellent projects. However, when providing opinions and making decisions, members need to take care that any dialogue is respectful.

Respectful Dialogue

VTMs are heavily engaged with their coworkers. As explained earlier in the context of understanding work ethics and applying critical thinking, not every comment is derogatory or requires an emotional response. VTMs should monitor their sensitivity levels, keeping an eye on the end goal. At the same time, VTMs should respect one another when providing project feedback. Commenting that "I don't like the background design" as opposed to saying "I think the background color should match the company's logo—what do you think?" makes a difference in how the message is perceived. Protocols should be followed for deliverables, so that when in doubt, VTMs can rely on process standards, only reporting major issues to the VTG.

Reviewing before Passing

VTMs should review and approve their own work and that of others as a team effort before approving it for the VTG to review. The VTG should be active and check work throughout the VTML process, but an informal pass review after the detailed review and engagement that have both been part of the feedback and work with other VTMs that consists of comments such as, "I think we covered every part of the deliverable, what do you think?" can be an acceptable expression of approval before the VTG formally reviews the deliverables and submits them to upper management. This ensures that the work is acceptable and of sufficient quality to submit to the next group in the VTML. All VTMs should review the deliverables they are working on before passing them on to the next group in the chain.

Don't Misuse Email

If major issues occur during teamwork, email may not be the correct way to respond, as explained earlier in this book. It's better to contact VTMs by voice-to-voice communication. To review work or troubleshoot, you can share files if necessary using tools such as DocSharing or Dropbox. For weekly emails to team members to keep everyone up to date, avoid verbose messages, but make it a habit to refer to make the status of the project clear in the subject line, for example:

> *"Done—Picture Stock Assessment"*
> *"In Progress—Picture Stock Assessment"*
> *"To Do—Picture Stock Assessment by Friday"*

As a VTM, the heart of the organization, it is better to over-communicate than to under-communicate when engaging with your coworkers at a distance. Such over-communication should not consist of taking several email messages to resolve issues, but instead using voice or some other type of verbal contact where communication is clearer. Consistency in this will matter, and will often be reciprocated by other VTMs, demonstrating interlocked communication.

OTHER BEST PRACTICES FOR VIRTUAL TEAM MEMBERS

Other best practices for VTMs include taking proper notes and organizing themselves. When working at a distance, VTMs need to develop a system that works for them. This might include the discipline to commit to hours to work with a mindset that deliverables must be accomplished or progressed during those periods, and keeping high-quality notes, perhaps using a spreadsheet, to track progress on personal deliverables. A method of organization is needed to ensure that interactions with other VTMs are followed through and mutual trust is fostered. To accomplish all this, VTMs may choose to create their own virtual offices.

What Does the Virtual Office Look Like?

Figuratively, the virtual office looks like a structural plan that includes the discipline required to do the work. This discipline includes being work-centered, exhibiting leadership qualities, maintaining good notes, and avoiding procrastination. Individuals working at a distance need a physical place to work where there are minimal distractions, whether in a home office or a room dedicated as a temporary office—this is obvious. But if they are not prepared mentally for work, nothing of quality will be accomplished.

Discipline
Can discipline be taught? Some people can naturally discipline themselves to work remotely, while others need consistent direction about what to do and what is expected. Not every employee is effective at working at a distance, and that's fine. Management have to decide on the types of skills employees need, and assess whether they are appropriate candidates for working at a distance. However, discipline requires motivation, time management skills, as mentioned above, and the ability to select the right protocols established by the company's rules or values when not being supervised directly. Management have to place trust in employees working at a distance, and that trust may be reflected in employees' self-discipline over time.

Discipline involves having a work-centered mindset. This doesn't mean that VTMs should only work or be consumed by work, but that they understand that it is necessary to allocate time to do high-quality work at a distance. Effective remote workers consider themselves good workers, and their work matters to them. A work-centered mindset consists of VTMs caring about their roles in the organization as a component of the whole virtual team project. VTMs who are not work-centered may view themselves as part-time employees—if not in reality, mentally—working at a distance, but not fully part of the organization. This is not meant to imply that part-time employees are not necessarily good workers, but that if VTMs believe that they do not matter to the organization, they will lack the discipline to be work-centered, resulting in their projects or deliverables being of substandard quality. Such VTMs may feel as if they are not really part of the team and that their deliverables do not mean as much as those of an employee working on the project in the company office, perhaps full-time, but definitely face-to-face with management. This will limit their roles in the virtual team, and they may end up seeing the technology involved as a barrier and feel inferior to employees in the brick and mortar organization.

Discipline also involves leadership. As noted above, individuals who naturally work well at a distance may be accustomed to leading and being more self-directed. More reliant members working at a distance may not be as comfortable with leadership roles, or may not fully understand how to take the lead in their own tasks. It is important for VTMs to understand that they do have leadership qualities and can create their own environment that places them in the driving seat or lets them serve as a teacher of virtual teamwork and deliverable completion. If VTMs adopt the attitude that they are the leaders of their personal deliverables and can explain what they are doing to other VTMs or VTGs, they take more power over their projects, their responsibilities, and their leadership skills.

Note-taking

Having a systematic method for keeping notes on deliverable progress, interaction with colleagues, and quick, accessible tracking of progress helps to create the VTM's personal virtual office. Notes should be clear and spaced out to enable quick reviewing. Details can be added at the end of the points or in a summary, but the main points should be clear statements. For example:

My Roles: Creating the television advertisements for the
    e-commerce project.
My Goals: Have draft of television advertisements and
    recommendations about quantity

- Draft created today—met task requirements.
- Spoke with VTM Reynolds, and feedback was fine but edits needed.
- Edits are made. Need more feedback/questions.

- Remote check-in today with VTG—prepare questions.
- Submitted deliverable to subgroup—need help with quantity.

Note-taking can include recording the main accomplishments during the day's work, supplementing the time management calendar. Drawing up lists of questions for the VTG and/or other VTMs at the end of the day is helpful as a reminder of what needs to be addressed and problems that need to be resolved. Effective note-taking leads to an organized office because it helps keep track of project needs and enables the VTM not only to ask relevant questions, but to answer those posed by other VTMs.

Procrastination
There will always be several tasks to complete, both personally and professionally. An excellent VTM will not lapse into procrastination. Procrastination is the nemesis of working at a distance. It is never a good idea to procrastinate on deliverables when working remotely. Other team members will be waiting for those deliverables, the VTM may lose track of updates and changes, and if sufficient time hasn't been allocated to work on deliverables, it will affect the entire project. Remember that what you present as a team member may influence what you receive as a team member. It is important to always keep in mind that procrastination will impede other team members' progress and eventually your own progress as an employee.

Since the team leader or project manager will be fully aware of the expected deliverables, having helped to design them, it should be relatively straightforward to check in with VTGs and specific VTMs if they need assistance in ensuring that deliverables and deadlines are met. Remote check-ins and synchronous meetings at different stages of deliverable development are essential. These allow VTGs and VTMs to communicate and voice their concerns, and this helps management to confirm that progress is being made and conflict is being managed.

Remote Check-in

Ideally, the remote check-in should take the form of a synchronous meeting involving team leaders or project managers, VTGs, and VTMs, and include Q&A sessions to troubleshoot any problems with deliverables. This allows VTMs to discuss any concerns about the project or individual concerns in an open forum, respectfully. Remote check-ins can consist of several meetings at different points in the project development process whenever VTGs or team leaders or project managers think they are necessary for deliverable improvement. They could occur as often as once a week or once a month, depending on the project and VTMs' needs. VTMs can also request remote-check-ins if necessary. If necessary, VTGs can also meet with VTMs to discuss deliverable progress without the participation of the team leader or project manager. During these meetings, Virtual Team Progress Forms can be assessed with general comments. Individual feedback on these forms should be provided to the VTMs privately, but general comments on where improvement and attention are needed for the project can demonstrate what is working and what needs more work at certain points during development. Ultimately, remote check-ins should be focused on the VTMs and helping them as they move along with deliverable progress, once again reassuring them that they are not alone when working at a distance.

O-SPAN YOUTH VTMS AT WORK ON DELIVERABLES

The teams have been structured and assigned, the deliverables are in progress, issues are being managed, and the VTG is checking in, keeping track of progress with notes in her Excel spreadsheet and submitting Virtual Team Progress Forms.

At this point, the virtual teams in North America, Latin America, and Europe are working on their deliverables. They have checked in with one another using O-Span Youth's virtual team software. Each team has been allocated deliverables, and Project Manager Daniels and VTG Roberts have communicated the specific deliverables each individual will complete. VTG Roberts uses her spreadsheet to track team progress and the expected deliverables.

1.   **Latin America and Europe are Working on the Database Design**

Table 4.3   Database design virtual teams

Latin America VTMs	Deliverable: database design	Status	Comments
Burrows	Main Designer	A	
Felix	Support Designer	A	
Garcia	Support Designer	A	
Garaphious	Support Designer	A	
Hannex	Support Designer	A	
Mantilla	Main Designer	A	
Micaelis	Support Designer	A	
Nicholas	Support Designer	A	

Note: In all the tables hereafter in this chapter, Virtual Team Presence Status Indicator: A = active, S = steady, N = needs improvement.

Europe VTMs	Deliverable: database design	Status	Comments
Abu	Support Designer	A	
Bain	Support Designer	A	
Derus	Support Designer	A	
Denim	Main Designer	A	
Hoxxy	Support Designer	A	
Kenard	Support Designer	A	
Williams	Support Designer	S	

Performance: The Main Designers, Burrows, Mantilla, and Denim, are setting up the mainframe for the database, and deliverables are coming along nicely. The Support Designers are ensuring that data exchange is compatible with all O-Span Youth's locations. There are some issues with foreign characters and query functions. Latin America seems to be taking the lead in troubleshooting. Main Designer Denim is fine with that, but wants to reassure the team that he is available to help if needed. He informs team members that he will work on some preliminaries to define the online transaction order process before they design it, so that he can maintain an active presence in the team.

Timeline: 2 months

VTG notes: The database template is ready for review. The Support Designers who are testing it, the VTG, and the Project Manager can now review its functionality.

2.   Latin America and Europe are Integrating Products

Table 4.4   Product integration virtual teams

Latin America VTMs	Deliverable: product integration	Status	Comments
Petrus	Marketer/Technical Lead	A	
Radolphus	Marketer	A	
Ricardus	Marketer/Technical	A	
Rogerus	Marketer/Technical	S	
Rosa A.	Marketer	S	
Rosa M.	Marketer	A	
Stephanus	Marketer	A	
Thomas	Marketer/Technical	S	
Tobias	Marketer	A	
Ursula	Marketer	A	
Wido	Marketer	A	
Wilomas	Marketer	A	
Xtopherus	Marketer	A	

Europe VTMs	Deliverable	Status	Comments
Abu	Support Designer	A	
Bain	Support Designer	A	
Derus	Support Designer	A	
Denim	Main Designer	A	
Hoxxy	Support Designer	A	
Kenard	Support Designer	A	
Williams	Support Designer	S	

Performance: Database testing went well. Product integration can now begin, since the database is functioning. Shoe products are identified for the first integration roll-out. Issues among the teams have emerged. Kenard communicates in a blunt manner, and Ursula has an issue with his communication style. She thinks he is too direct and critical about her work. She has emailed a few of her fellow VTMs about the issue, and one of the emails was forwarded to Kenard. Kenard responds to Ursula with the following message:

To: Ursula

> *"I was forwarded the email in which you felt obliged to insult my character. Not only is this demeaning to me, but now you have tainted others' views on our teams. I am not working to appease you; my concern is the bottom-line product. Your work is substandard. I ask that if you have an issue with my communication, address me, not the team."*

Ursula is offended by the email and interaction with Kenard. She forwards the email to VTG Roberts, requesting an intervention.

Roberts is disturbed that this pettiness is distracting from accomplishing the deliverable, but wants to acknowledge Ursula's concerns. Roberts calls Kenard and informs him that she is reviewing deliverables from all VTMs, and that insulting his teammates is counterproductive. He is welcome to provide feedback, but not feedback that is personally insulting. Although Kenard is thereafter more cautious in interaction with his peers, he still communicates directly, but not with insults. He apologizes to Ursula.

Timeline: 1 Month

VTG notes: Roberts submits VTG Progress Forms. She approves the roll-out of products. The IT team is completing full integration. Roberts is pleased with the deliverables and places them in the communal e-room where other VTMs can access them. Robert sends out a weekly memo reminding VTMs to check in regularly and acknowledge memos.

3. **Latin America and Europe are Creating the Online Transaction Order Process**

Table 4.5   Online transaction order virtual teams

Latin America VTMs	Deliverable: online order process	Status	Comments
Burrows	Main Designer	A	
Felix	Support Designer	A	
Garcia	Support Designer	A	
Garaphious	Support Designer	A	
Hannex	Support Designer	A	
Mantilla	Main Designer	A	
Micaelis	Support Designer	A	
Nicholas	Support Designer	A	

Europe VTMs	Deliverable: online order process	Status	Comments
Abu	Support Designer	A	
Bain	Support Designer	A	
Derus	Support Designer	A	
Denim	Main Designer	A	
Hoxxy	Support Designer	A	
Kenard	Support Designer	A	
Williams	Support Designer	S	

Performance: The teams are progressing well with the online order transaction process, but VTG Roberts has observed from the Virtual Team Progress Forms that there are some members who need to improve their communication. Deliverables are still being delivered, so the slow progress is not having an obvious effect on deadlines until Roberts's remote check-in, when she discovers some issues.

Remote check-in

VTG Roberts does her remote check-in with the teams and discovers some conflict concerns that are starting to escalate and impact deliverables. The Latin America team is experiencing issues with the Europe team about e-transaction order development. VTM Williams on the Europe team has not submitted his edits to the order process.

Meanwhile, VTMs Hannex and Felix on the Latin America virtual teams are commenting that their ideas are not being received well by their teams. Hannex and Felix seem to be the only VTMs with concerns about the inability to make seamless changes to the design when new products are added for future e-commerce projects. Following the current plan and members' specifications, there may be problems with customers' orders if components are not implemented during the initial design.

Roberts has to intervene. First, she contacts Williams by telephone and receives a voice mail message from him. She leaves a message asking him to contact her, and follows up with the following email message:

> *"Your virtual team response time on the e-commerce project is a concern. Members are waiting on your edits to proceed. Please submit by the end of the week, and contact me with any questions."*

The next resolution approach implemented by Roberts consists of documenting the concerns of Hannex and Felix and consulting with Daniels about them, since this issue may affect both teams working on the order process. Daniels contacts management and subject matter experts to assess Hannex's and Felix's viewpoints at this stage in the project's progress. The discussions and research result in adding functionality that is cost-effective and within budget that allows more seamless accommodation of new products. Daniels hosts a meeting with Roberts and the database design teams to discuss the new integration and team impacts and deliverables. Hannex and Felix are commended for their actions by management, and Roberts sends out a memo after the meeting informing all teams about the add-ons.

Timeline: 1 month

VTG notes: Now that the template is ready and products have been integrated, testing of the order transaction process that has been created can begin.

4.   **North America Defines Marketing Tools**

Table 4.6   North America marketing virtual teams— marketing tools

North America VTMs	Deliverable: marketing tools	Status	Comments
Bibbs	Marketer Blog Contacts	A	
Bouse	Marketer Social Media	A	
Collins	Marketer Social Media	A	Re-check
Christos	Marketer Televisions	A	
Davis	Marketer Blog Contacts	A	
Eaton	Marketer Blog Contacts	A	
Earls	Marketer Television	S	Check in?
Reynolds	Marketer Television	A	

Performance: VTMs Bibbs, Davis, and Eaton are checking in with one another to complete the blog contact deliverables. VTMs Bouse and Collins are working on the virtual team software to complete the social media deliverable. VTMs

Christos, Earls, and Reynolds are working on completing the television media deliverable.

Timeline: 1 Month

VTG notes: The blogs and social media deliverables have been completed, and the VTMs have submitted them for review. The television deliverables are not ready yet. VTG Roberts has assigned Bouse to help Christos, Earls, and Reynolds. Television marketing will now meet its deadline. Roberts submits Virtual Team Progress Forms, approves the North America marketing tools, and places the deliverables in the e-room for other teams to access.

5. North America Creates Online Advertising Campaign

Table 4.7   North America marketing virtual teams— online advertising campaign

North America VTMs	Deliverable: online advertising campaign	Status	Comments
Bibbs	Marketer Blog Contacts	A	
Bouse	Marketer Social Media	A	
Collins	Marketer Social Media	A	Re-check
Christos	Marketer Television	A	
Davis	Marketer Blog Contacts	A	
Eaton	Marketer Blog Contacts	A	
Earls	Marketer Television	S	Check in?
Reynolds	Marketer Television	A	

Performance: VTMs feel enthusiastic about the online advertising campaign created for O-Span Youth's new e-commerce website, and are satisfied with progress on deliverables.

Timeline: 1 month

VTG notes: E-marketing literature and promotions are ready for review by all teams and have been placed in the e-room.

6. **North America, Europe, and Latin America Develop E-partnerships**

Table 4.8   E-partnerships virtual teams

North America VTMs	Deliverable: e-partnerships	Status	Comments
Collins	Marketer	A	
Christos	Marketer	A	
Davis	Marketer	A	
Eaton	Marketer	A	

Latin America VTMs	Deliverable: e-partnerships	Status	Comments
Petrus	Marketer	A	
Radolphus	Marketer/PR Lead	A	
Ricardus	Marketer	A	
Rogerus	Marketer	A	
Rosa M.	Marketer	N	
Stephanus	Marketer	A	

Europe VTMs	Deliverable: e-partnerships	Status	Comments
Aberlard	Marketer	A	
Baccus	Marketer	A	
Divens	Marketer/Production Specialist	A	
Durand	Marketer	A	
Halls	Marketer	A	
Jolly	Marketer	A	

Performance: The North America, Europe, and Latin America teams are checking in using the virtual team software. They are engaging with their peers by posting messages in threads about deliverables and progress. Collins sends an email to Eaton saying that he is concerned that the Europe VTMs are not progressing well. They have posted messages about their intentions regarding the deliverable, but there have been no resulting e-partnerships. With a month to go before the expected delivery time, Collins is concerned that the draft deadline will not be met. Collins then contacts Radolphus, the PR Lead, and determines that some of the e-markets have not signed on to advertise with O-Span Youth, which is the cause of the delay. Collins is just about to contact VTG Roberts when Roberts sends out a memo stating that some of the e-markets did not decide to partner and that the e-commerce project is moving forward.

Timeline: 1 month

VTG notes: E-market listing and active e-partnerships have been secured. The results are below expectations, but fortunately Web banners and advertisements have been secured with five top e-marketers. O-Span Youth's marketing team will need to keep working on marketing.

7.   Europe Creates Specialty Products

Table 4.9   Specialty products virtual teams

Europe VTMs	Deliverable: specialty products	Status	Comments
Aberlard	Designer/Graphics Technical Lead	A	
Baccus	Designer	A	
Divens	Designer	A	
Durand	Designer	A	

Halls	Designer/Graphics Technical Lead	A	
Jolly	Designer/Graphics Technician	A	
Knight	Designer	S	
Lane	Designer/Graphics Technician	A	
Limon	Designer	A	
Turner	Designer	A	

Performance: The Europe VTMs have several deliverables to complete that are similar to those of the Latin America team. Along with database design, they have dispersed members working on customer service deliverables. VTG Roberts has assigned teams to complete the deliverables.

Timeline: 1 month

VTG notes: Specialty product unique identifiers have been created. Roll-out is ready, and they have been placed in the e-room for review.

8.   **Latin America and Europe Set Up Customer Service Support**

Table 4.10   Technical virtual teams

Europe VTMs	Deliverable: customer service	Status	Comments
Abu	Support Designer	A	
Bain	Support Designer	A	
Derus	Support Designer	A	
Denim	Main Designer	A	
Hoxxy	Main Designer	A	
Kenard	Support Designer	A	
Williams	Support Designer	S	

Latin America VTMs	Deliverable: online order process	Status	Comments
Burrows	Main Designer	A	
Felix	Support Designer	A	
Garcia	Support Designer	A	
Garaphious	Support Designer	A	
Hannex	Main Designer	A	
Mantilla	Main Designer	A	
Micaelis	Support Designer	A	
Nicholas	Support Designer	A	

Performance: The teams are progressing well on their deliverables. VTG Roberts is pleased with progress, but has decided to use subgroups to close the gaps and help progress to flow more quickly and effectively.

Timeline: 1 month

VTG notes: The 24-hour customer support team has been established.

9. **Latin America and Europe Set Up Phone Support for E-commerce Customers**

Table 4.11 Phone support virtual teams

Europe VTMs	Deliverable: phone support	Status	Comments
Causette	Main Designer	A	
Menard	Main Designer	A	
Wofu	Main Designer	A	
Zeran	Support Designer	A	
Zox	Support Designer	A	

Latin America VTMs	Deliverable: phone support	Status	Comments
Burrows	Main Designer	A	
Felix	Support Designer	A	
Garcia	Support Designer	A	

Performance: The e-commerce phone support setup teams encounter a few challenges with the roll-out of the phone systems. Burrows, Mantilla, and Abu contact VTG Roberts to ask for more subject matter experts to be assigned to assist them. The Support Designers have been active, but Roberts needs Project Manager Daniels's expertise to resolve this issue. Daniels outsources two subject matter expert individuals to help the teams establish the Web-based phone service connections.

Timeline: 1 month

VTG notes: All systems are in place. Subject matter experts have helped the team to roll out the deliverables.

10. **Latin America and Europe Create Automated Data Collection System**

Table 4.12   Technical data team virtual teams

Latin America VTMs	Deliverable: data collection	Status	Comments
Burrows	Main Designer	A	
Felix	Support Designer	A	
Garcia	Main Designer	A	
Garaphious	Support Designer	A	
Hannex	Support Designer	A	
Mantilla	Main Designer	A	
Micaelis	Support Designer	A	
Nicholas	Support Designer	A	

Europe VTMs	Deliverable: customer service	Status	Comments
Abu	Main Designer	A	
Bain	Support Designer	A	
Derus	Support Designer	A	
Denim	Main Designer	A	
Hoxxy	Support Designer	A	
Kenard	Support Designer	A	
Williams	Support Designer	S	

Performance: Teams members are generally active. Data capture applications have been installed, and testing has begun.

Timeline: 1 month

VTG notes: Data automation needs an extended series of tests, so the teams are close to deadline for their deliverables. VTG Roberts contacts Daniels about her deadline concerns. Fortunately, additional time has been allocated to allow for such issues, so the testing time should be fine.

COMMUNICATION PHASE 3

Having consistently checked in with their VTGs and the team leader or project manager, the teams are ready for a detailed review of their deliverables—it is time for Communication Phase 3.

Communication Phase 3

Communication Phase 3 consists of an assessment of deliverables, and may include testing to ensure that the project deliverables are ready for management review and submission. Communication Phase 3 consists another synchronous meeting or a series of meetings. Each communication phase can consist of several parts if necessary, depending on the project. Part 1 of Communication Phase 3 could include a review of deliverables for specific departments. Part 2 of Communication Phase 3 could consist of testing to ensure that all systems are in place and functioning before management reviews the product, followed by a meeting to discuss the results. Part 3 of Communication Phase 3 could consist of a final meeting involving all team members to pursue any updates or issues. Ideally, the team leader or project manager will review the deliverables submitted at this point. He or she should have full access to the virtual team software to review deliverables continuously during the project development process and stay in contact with the VTG throughout the project. At this point, the team leader or project manager can offer any final suggestions or edits.

In Part 1, the team leader or project manager may choose meet with just the VTG or VTMs working on the database design or the creative team to enable a clear. The next stage can include testing followed by a meeting to discuss the results, or a meeting involving all groups to discuss deliverable completion. VTMs can then work on any edits resulting from Communication Phase 3 and all its parts. Reviews by the team leader or project manager and reports on testing are necessary throughout the project, but Communication Phase 3 should be the final testing stage, and minimal edits should be required.

Communication Phase 3 is the final stage in the VTML, ending with everyone involved signing off on the project and presenting the deliverables to management.

Project Submission

CHAPTER 4: REVIEW

The *virtual team guide* has several responsibilities. As explained in the VTML, these include keeping the team leader or project manager updated on any issues and the progress of the virtual teams. The virtual team guide is responsible for helping virtual team members to work cohesively, and this role may be taken on by more than one person depending on the number of virtual teams required for the project. Other duties include organizing *weekly check-ins* and handling some of the deliverable responsibilities, as well as *conflict management*. Conflict management may consist of arbitrating disagreements among members, ensuring that process standards are being met and deliverables are of a high quality. Virtual team guides submit reviews via *Virtual Team Progress Forms* to virtual team members so that they can evaluate their own progress.

Virtual team members are the remote workers ultimately responsible for the deliverables. They are the hands-on workers who have to collaborate and communicate with their coworkers to produce the projects, products, and tangible items that constitute the deliverables. Virtual team members have to adopt a *critical thinking* mindset when working at a distance to deal with *conflict* and *time management*. With regard to critical thinking, virtual team members must accept that others may have different work ethics, learning styles, and response styles that influence remote team dynamics and personal reactions to scenarios that may crop up when working at a distance.

Technological advances mean that virtual team members have a range of options available to help them resolve problems and engage with their coworkers online. Virtual team members and virtual team guides can have opportunities to express their concerns and issues about deliverables via consistent *remote check-in Q&A sessions.* *Communication Phase 3* allows for a review and assessment of deliverables. If all systems are in place and the deliverables are of the quality required, the project can then be submitted to management.

O-SPAN YOUTH'S COMMUNICATION PHASE 3

VTG Roberts submits the deliverables for approval to Project Manager Daniels. Daniels reviews the files and sets up Communication Phase 3 meetings for feedback. Roberts congratulates the VTMs on a job well done, and feels confident that the deliverables are ready for management to review.

Project Submission: CEO Wilcox is pleased with the project. O-Span's e-commerce website is operating smoothly, and sales have expanded in the first year.

BUSINESS APPLICATIONS OF THE VIRTUAL TEAM GLOBAL BUSINESS MODEL

INTRODUCING PRACTICAL BUSINESS APPLICATIONS USING THE VIRTUAL TEAM GLOBAL BUSINESS MODEL

This chapter discusses how practical use of the Virtual Team Global Business Model (see Figure 5.1) is effective for business professionals who are managing remote workers. The practical uses include engaging with virtual teams, managing cultural differences, applying process standards (as previewed in Chapter 1), and managing virtual teams across multiple locations. It can be applied to both companies and higher education establishments (discussed in Chapter 6) that are using virtual teams to complete projects, whether the participants are working at a distance in the organization's office or in their home offices.

Chronos Consulting, a company focused on significantly improving its clients' performance in a range of areas, conducted a survey on the projected usage of virtual teams. It contacted 1,764 companies in the US and Canada by telephone, and 83 surveys were completed by their employees: 57 percent of the companies reported that they planned to use virtual teams more in the future, and 72 percent mentioned cost reduction as the primary reason for doing so.[1]

---

1   These data and "The Top Eight Benefits of Virtual/Mobile Workforces Across Industries in North America" at the end of this chapter are based on a survey conducted on virtual teams by Chronos Consulting in 2011 (*The State of Virtual Team Utilization in the 21st Century*, www.chronosconsulting.org/dl/Virtual-Teams-Utilization-Research-Survey-Sep-1-2011.pdf, accessed December 17, 2013).

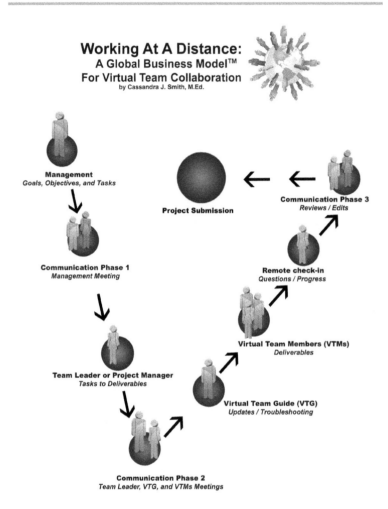

Figure 5.1   Virtual Team Global Business Model™

Chronos Consulting specializes in significantly improving business results for organizations, particularly in the areas of performance improvement, global, cross-functional, and virtual team building, supply chain and human capital management, and shared services. Its goal is to assist clients in achieving breakthrough business results within compressed timeframes, with a guaranteed return on investment. For more information, visit www.chronosconsulting.org, or call 1-800-331-1350.

Working at a distance can be cost-effective for businesses. The VTML provides practical tools for managing multiple business sites and enables management to be active in virtual teams. If virtual teams are left to their own devices, issues can ensue that are uncontrollable. With more companies using virtual teams, the VTML aims to develop more practical methods for communicating at a distance and a system to help enhance effective collaboration, with management taking a strong role. We will now address the questions of what high-quality collaboration looks like in terms of process standards, and how this relates to the VTML.

HIGH-QUALITY COLLABORATION AND PROCESS STANDARDS

Process standards are guidelines and specifications that apply to businesses, and in this instance, virtual team collaboration. Process standards can help to close virtual team performance gaps because employees and management understand what is expected of them when collaborating remotely. In high-quality collaboration, VTMs are active and understand the challenges of working at a distance, but realize that commitment to the project can overcome these. This strong commitment results from the perception that management cares, so VTMs understand that the project is a priority, that they are not alone when working at a distance, and that their management are invested in the process—all this establishes mutual trust. Substandard collaboration results when VTMs are left to figure out processes for themselves as they proceed with the project, which can lead to lackadaisical attitudes toward working remotely.

Process standards can also consist of skills that need to be developed in order for high-quality collaboration to take place. For example, the Virtual Team Skills Assessment Forms can establish whether some VTMs do not enjoy working in teams or prefer to work autonomously, in which case a process standard might consist of educating members about what it means to work collaboratively and how respectful dialogue and diverse opinions can be positive in virtual teams.

Even VTMs who may not normally enjoy working in teams can be coached to collaborate effectively if clear process standards with a focus on high-quality collaboration are in place.

THE VTML AND PROCESS STANDARDS

In the Virtual Team Global Business Model, management are the driving force behind developing process standards. Clear communication begins at the top of the employment chain, and flows down to all levels. Management are responsible for defining process standards for the entire project. This is logical, since management can see the whole picture at the beginning of the project. The team leader or project manager is then responsible for defining process standards for the virtual team guide, who in turn is responsible for conveying them to the virtual team members. If management feel that defining the process standards for the entire project will benefit from insight from subject matter experts, their assistance should be enlisted. The point of quality process standards is to ensure that all bases are covered to ensure the integrity of the project, to protect the company's reputation for delivering high-quality goods and services, and to establish systems to solicit feedback from VTMs to improve the performance of virtual teams.

Management Defining Process Standards

Management are responsible for setting process standards for the entire project, as they define the goals, objectives, and tasks for the project to be accomplished by their virtual teams. From management's point of view, process standards range from the integrity of the design to communication efforts. As stated above, high-quality process standards include three important elements: the integrity of the project, the company's reputation for delivering high-quality goods and services, and systems for gathering feedback from all those involved.

The integrity of the project
Process standards that boost the integrity of the project demonstrate management's active involvement. Management must be honest and sincere about the intent of the project so that employees can in turn be honest and care about the design and each element they contribute. Management should compose focused goals, objectives, and tasks that are not complicated in nature and that highlight the value of the project to the company. Most employees understand that their jobs are more secure when they adhere to policies, but polices and process standards should be based on integrity and values.

The company's reputation for high-quality goods and services
If a company has loyal customers and a reputation for delivering high-quality goods and services, it will be easier for it to attract new customers. Word of mouth, the Internet, and customer satisfaction are catalysts that help to secure this reputation. However, if VTMs are unaware of process standards while they are working and creating their deliverables for projects, the company's reputation will be in jeopardy. For example, a cumbersome ordering process that intimidates customers visiting a website could result from a worker not understanding the process standards for development. If management never conveyed process standards regarding integrity of design or thought that those process standards had been conveyed despite a lack of clear documentation, customers will avoid visiting the site because of ordering problems. Process standards relating to the quality of goods and services must be a prime consideration when management utilize virtual teams to complete projects.

Feedback from employees
As stated above, there needs to be documentary evidence from each employee, whether working at a distance or face-to-face, to confirm that they understand the required process standards. Speaking with team leaders or project managers to verify that process standards have been conveyed, getting employees to sign paperwork setting out the process standards, and providing them with opportunities to ask questions if they are unsure about process standards are ways to ensure they have been communicated properly. Encouraging employees to discuss their

concerns with management at any point in the production process is a value-added service for management and employees working at a distance. Often managers are busy and do not allocate sufficient time to dealing with their remote workers, projects, and participating in Q&A sessions. This is a huge mistake on management's part. If virtual team projects are to be successful, process standards must be clearly defined and adhered to, and employees need reassurance that management cares about the project.

How Can Process Standards be Set Up to Meet these Three Criteria?

Continuing our description of the O-Span Youth e-commerce project, here are some examples of process standards that could be defined by management for each department working on distance projects.

Information Technology Virtual Teams:

- Refer to the IT testing plan for database evaluation.
- Formal statements of IT specifications must be submitted.
- Adhere to the integrity of the design at stated in O-Span Youth's policies and procedures.
- Use Quality Assurance tools for testing.
- Submit project/employee evaluations at the end of the project.
- If in doubt about any process standard or expectation in this category, contact your supervisor.

Marketing Virtual Teams:

- Present marketing material with credibility (see O-Span Youth's Marketing Ethics and Policies Forms).
- Adhere to the marketing principles established by O-Span Youth's policies and procedures.
- Approval of marketing materials must be granted by your supervisor.

- Submit project/employee evaluations at the end of the project.
- If in doubt about any process standard or expectation in this category, contact your supervisor.

Business E-partnerships Virtual Teams:

- You must explain the non-competition clause and secure the appropriate signatures from the e-partners.
- Distributors of O-Span Youth's products globally must follow contractual guidelines.
- Submit project/employee evaluations at end of the project.
- If in doubt about any process standard or expectation in this category, contact your supervisor.

Customer Service Virtual Teams:

- Accuracy in customers' orders must be the top priority.
- Response time to customers must not exceed O-Span Youth's 24 hours policy.
- Customers' issues must be resolved respectfully and by being accommodating, within reason.
- Submit project/employee evaluations at end of the project.
- If in doubt about any process standard or expectation in this category, contact your supervisor.

Management will benefit from appointing individuals to ensure that the process standards are being met and that data is collected as specified by some of these standards. If the team leader or project manager is not fully cognizant with some of the areas, it is a good idea for management to allocate other employees in leadership positions to take on the roles, or alternatively use the company's quality control or inventory control department to manage all its process standards. Each team or department working at a distance must have process standards that include evaluations, as in the example above to garner employee feedback (evaluations will be discussed in more detail in Chapter 6). Project and employee evaluations must be part of each process standard, as must the direction to contact the supervisor if there is any doubt about process standards.

Team Leaders or Project Managers Defining Process Standards

Team leaders or project managers are responsible for working with the virtual team guide(s) and virtual team members to ensure that deliverable targets are being met and that they are of sufficient quality to submit to management. Team leaders or project managers are the bridge between top-level management and employees working on virtual projects. They will try to resolve any conflicts and locate resources or subject matter experts, and also assist the VTGs in supporting the VTMs. Conveying process standards from the team leader or project manager to the VTG aids in the development process, and ranges from ensuring accountability to setting check-points.

Returning to the O-Span Youth e-commerce project, here are some examples of process standards for the VTG that could be defined by the team leader or project manager:

- Ensure that Virtual Team Progress Forms are provided for each employee.
- Confirm that conflict management strategies are in place.
- Provide regular meetings, webinars, and Q&A sessions for the VTMs.
- Keep the e-room updated with the latest Standard Operating Procedures.

Team leaders or project managers will ensure that deliverables are of the required quality before they are presented to upper management. This depends on their VTGs and VTMs, so process standards to support communication among the VTGs and VTMs are vital. Team leaders or project managers bear the ultimate responsibility for accomplishing the stated objectives and ensuring that deliverable targets are met.

If their VTGs or VTMs are having issues and the distance project is suffering as a result, team leaders or project managers are responsible for resolving the problems; the process standards set by management mean they bear the bulk of the responsibility for any shortfalls or project complications.

Virtual Team Guides Defining Process Standards

In the VTML, virtual team guides are responsible for working directly with the virtual team members, serving as the go-to individual for help and project concerns. VTGs have to devise VTM process standards that allow them to manage their virtual teams effectively to meet their own process standards. The VTG's process standards for VTMs may be general or specific depending on the needs of the virtual teams, and may range from communication guidelines to helping to create a sense of security rather than isolation for team members working remotely.

Returning again to the O-Span Youth project, here are some examples of process standards that could be defined by the VTG:

- Follow O-Span's Work Quality Design for Project Development.
- Be open to providing and receiving respectful feedback.
- Be consistent in your responses to coworkers.
- Refer to the Conflict Management Protocol defined by the VTG.
- Refer to the Communication E-Flow Document for guidance.
- Adhere to the Proxy Protocol if you will be unavailable on a work day.
- Ask for help at any stage of development if you need it, particularly if the issues may affect deliverables due dates.

The VTG serves as a facilitator, and facilitation regarding process standards includes issuing updates and setting communication check-points throughout the project development process. Holding regular meetings and constantly ensuring that employees have the latest versions of files and information can make significant differences to the outcome of a project. VTGs must be active, not only by holding meetings and issuing updates, but helping to complete deliverables if team members are slacking or simply need assistance. The VTG has a huge task that should driven by a focus on the outcome of deliverables. The role can be so demanding that it is advisable to appoint more than one VTG when managing multiple sites.

MULTIPLE VIRTUAL TEAM MANAGEMENT

Administering virtual teams across multiple locations is no easy feat for management, requiring intensive communication with other managers and employees to oversee the process. The VTML presents a structure and timelines for management to follow to enhance involvement with their virtual teams in different locations during the various phases of the project. Often in virtual teams project, managers tend not to be as involved. Management is defined as overseeing, organizing, leading, guiding, administering, and demonstrating. For remote projects, this means avoiding technology-driven viewpoints, and adopting people-driven approaches to the use of technology.

Managers may be too preoccupied with day-to-day operations to prioritize their virtual teams. They may not check in regularly with their teams, and may fail to participate for various reasons. Managers may not understand how to fulfill their role effectively when working at a distance. They may assume that their remote workers understand how to work in virtual teams when this isn't the case. They may not appreciate the value of remote workers. Managing multiple site locations demands organization and leadership. The VTML is a guide that management can apply to develop viable remote work methods across multiple site locations.

The VTML and Multiple Site Management

Management
The first step in the VTML is for management to define the goals, objectives, and tasks. A team of managers in different locations can be involved in this process. The CEO or manager overseeing this step can bring all the managers together in a synchronous or face-to-face meeting to clarify the importance of the remote project. Establishing rapport and an approach for the virtual team project will help to connect everyone in upper management who will ultimately lead this project at the different sites.

Communication Phase 1
Managing multiple sites calls for several communication phases. Since the managers as a group will already be familiar with the goals, objectives, and tasks because they were responsible for defining them, the Communication Phase 1 meeting should include the team leaders or project managers who will be involved, and explain the parameters for the project to them. The managers should express their commitment to coaching and monitoring the virtual teams and adopting an active role. They will ensure that all employees are trained to use the software required, which entails allocating a budget for this. A skills assessment should be conducted for all employees working remotely, whether home-based or in the company's offices. All of this should not just be lipservice. These are vital steps in managing multiple sites.

For global teams, management must ensure that they provide the proper software and pay attention to cultural needs. It is extremely important for management to be culturally sensitive. Communication Phase 1 should include all the leaders in all the locations where the virtual teams will be located. There are a variety of issues that often afflict managing virtual teams across dispersed locations, and the VTML can help to ameliorate many of them.

Cultural Concerns

Cultural concerns are a major issue that can reflect the differences rather than the camaraderie among team members. They can include the ways members communicate, such as being open versus reticent, skill sets, such as being stronger in technology than another group, and ways of resolving conflict, such as being trustful, confrontational, or remaining silent. Some members may alienate those from other cultures to the point where the other VTMs feel that they are being too assertive and demanding on the project. This can impact management significantly, causing serious issues to arise if not addressed. Adults generally do not respond well to demands, especially demands from peers. Active management will not allow this to happen, and cultural groups working at a distance will not feel marginalized if management has addressed cultural issues from the start of the project. If branches of the business are located throughout the world, a wise manager will ensure that management teams and VTMs from these areas are included in the virtual team project.

Using the Virtual Team Skills Assessment to establish the daily cultural activities of each group involved may prove helpful. Attitudes to these activities should be inclusive wherever possible, but establishing a conflict management system and check-points to allow concerns to be aired can help in managing cultural differences. The main point is that it is not appropriate to seek to change a foreign culture: that would be foolish, and could be disastrous. A more prudent approach is to present different ideas and perspectives that may lead individuals to decide whether an approach, idea, or resolution will work.

Time Zones

Time zones can be problematic when managing and participating in geographically dispersed virtual teams. Some members may be logging off for the day while others are logging on. Technology must be provided that accommodates the various virtual teams, such as instant chat programs allowing for quick responses between members in different time zones. Another consideration about working across time zones is that management should take them into account when forming the teams. Demanding designs or deliverables may progress more efficiently if they are allocated to members collaborating within the same or closely related time zones. Diversity can still be represented within the teams, but management must be realistic and have a clear idea of which employees in different locations will be able to complete the project successfully.

Team leaders or project managers
In multiple site management, the team leaders or project managers converting tasks into deliverables may also be geographically dispersed. This is another area where it is important to take time zones into account, because many of these activities can be undertaken autonomously before collaborating with other team leaders or project managers. For example, a leader in a site in Latin America could convert tasks to deliverables that his or her team will complete for the IT department, whereas a leader in a site in North America could convert tasks to deliverables for his or her marketing department. The groups involved can discuss the deliverables collaboratively and help one another as needed. Managing multiple sites requires connectedness, whereby each site is fully aware of what other sites are working on.

Communication Phase 2
When interacting with multiple sites, the same applies to Communication Phase 2. This synchronous meeting may be large, because it needs to include team leaders or project managers, VTGs, and VTMs from all the different sites involved. The review of deliverables should be the main focus during this meeting. To make the meeting more manageable, Communication Phase 2 could be broken down into a series of meeting to introduce the deliverables to the various teams. Following the initial meeting or meetings, team leaders or project managers can choose to hold several further meetings involving VTMs, incorporating Q&A sessions and ensuring more effective management of the teams from the start.

VTGs

VTGs working across multiple sites can meet with other VTGs in a similar way to management. This is pertinent to the way the deliverables will flow and how interrelated they are to one another. VTGs have to stay in contact and communicate frequently with the other VTGs so that all the teams are kept up to date on deliverable progress, issues, contingencies, and updates. The VTGs need to keep the team leaders or project managers informed about the status of deliverables. Most importantly, the VTGs are responsible for the daily operations of the virtual teams. They need to motivate, resolve conflicts, and help with deliverables, ensuring that they continue to progress.

Remote check-ins are an excellent way for VTGs to provide feedback to VTMs across multiple site locations. Holding several synchronous meeting can reaffirm that the project is important, is proceeding satisfactorily, and that concerns will be addressed. Remote check-ins should not only consist of VTGs speaking and conducting reviews; the active participation of VTMs should be a priority, and every effort should be made to reassure them that their needs are being recognized.

VTMs

Out of all the groups involved, virtual team members may experience more difficulties than any other when working across multiple locations for reasons touched upon earlier, such as problems ensuring that everyone is participating, contact with some of their coworkers leading to misunderstandings, different understandings of expectations, issues with accepting responsibility for deliverables, avoiding the duplication of deliverables, and garnering feedback. VTMs should check in with their counterparts three or more times a day as they work to complete deliverables across multiple sites. Some issues that occur during distance work can be alleviated by a strong management presence as described by the VTML.

Communication Phase 3

The final phase of the project and the VTML before project submission consists of management meeting with all the groups to review the deliverables. When multiple sits are involved, Communication Phase 3 may consist of several meetings and testing stages to ensure that project and process standards have been met. Management can meet with other managers and leaders to assess the project, then eventually close out the deliverables, if accepted, then close out the entire project as finally completed, at which point the ultimate goal is achieved: project submission.

MANAGING VIRTUAL TEAMS WITH TECHNOLOGY

Managing virtual teams requires consistency, whether the teams include workers located in a company office or in another country. Management must be active and allocate time for virtual teamwork as they would any other task that makes their company unique and outstanding. The VTML encourages management to be present and to help build synergy within virtual teams. Virtual team members move along in harmony when management manages virtual teams effectively.

People-driven, Not Technology-driven

As noted earlier, the VTML is people-driven, not technology-driven. The wide range of Web-based technologies and portable computing devices such as iPads, laptops, cellular phones and other facilities that enable communication that are available nowadays make it much easier for VTMs to work together. However, these technologies must not supplant the human element of contacting VTMs voice-to-voice when necessary.

Another key point regarding managing virtual teams is that technical training is important—as explained in the "Skills Assessment" section in Chapter 3. If employees don't have up-to-date software knowledge, communicating and working on deliverables can be challenging. Needless to say, all employees should be trained to use the company's software to interact with others in their teams, but other tools such as Skype that allow for face time should also be part of the training. It is vital to provide adequate communication tools to enable VTMs to contact and work collaboratively with each other, but it is also a good idea to require VTMs to adhere to certain online office hours when they are available to other VTMs. A regular slot for a video chat or instant messaging chat once a week allows for interpersonal connections that supplement the other check-in points and communication phases included in the VTML.

CHAPTER 5: REVIEW

Working across multiple geographically dispersed site locations can be taxing, not least for management, who have to be present in all the virtual teams involved. Establishing well thought out systems to achieve this can make the difference between a high-quality and a substandard virtual team project. *Process standards* are guidelines and specifications governing the business and the integrity of the projects. High-quality collaboration ensures that members are active because they understand the expectations from the start of the project.

Management define process standards for the project as a whole, then team leaders or project managers define process standards for the VTGs, and the VTGs then define process standards for VTMs. Process standards help to clarify VTMs' responsibilities and provide opportunities for them to give feedback about their challenges when working at a distance on specific deliverables. Process standards include forms, protocols, and communication strategies for all remote workers, solidifying expectations when working at a distance.

Multiple location management involves managers communicating with and being active in all their virtual teams. Being aware of *cultural issues, time zones,* and ways to connect remote workers using *technology* helps to ensure that communication among all participants is consistent and none fall by the wayside. Effective multiple location management enables employees and employers to share content and ideas, establish relationships, and work cohesively at a distance.

THE TOP EIGHT BENEFITS OF VIRTUAL/MOBILE WORKFORCES ACROSS INDUSTRIES IN NORTH AMERICA

1. **Productivity improvement**—Virtual/mobile workers can save time by working from home or other convenient locations, becoming more productive while taking reduced sick time.

2. **Lower labor costs**—Because salaries vary by geography, employers using virtual workforces can hire workers in less costly labor markets, saving money.

3. **Reduced expenses**—The cost of hiring virtual employees is much lower than dedicated office space. In addition, eliminating rent, taxes, and utility expenses can result in significant savings.

4. **Reduced travel expenses**—Improved virtual meeting technology and tools (audio/video/Web conferencing, Skype, and so on) have facilitated the use of virtual conferences, which has reduced travel expenses considerably for companies.

5. **Wider talent pool**—Employers with virtual workforces are not limited to employees in their local area, enabling them to hire highly qualified workers from around the world.

6. **Happier employees**—Virtual employees are typically more amenable to working more often, which can help accommodate workload fluctuations. Having employees work virtually on projects with increased global risk can create a better work/life balance.

7. **Reduced employee turnover**—Employees who are more content are likely to stay with a company for a longer period of time. Because labor costs make up a large portion of the operating budget for many organizations, reducing turnover can lower operational expenses.

8. **Hiring employees with flexible circumstances and/or disabilities**—Employees with disabilities, unique situations, or work-oriented limitations due to special circumstances (maternity/paternity/eldercare leave) can be utilized as virtual workers. This can be of mutual benefit for companies, which can get access to a valuable pool of workers that would otherwise be difficult or perhaps impossible to reach.

Source: Chronos Consulting (2011), *The State of Virtual Team Utilization in the 21st Century*, www.chronosconsulting.org/dl/Virtual-Teams-Utilization-Research-Survey-Sep-1-2011.pdf (accessed December 17, 2013).

HIGHER EDUCATION AND THE VIRTUAL TEAM GLOBAL BUSINESS MODEL

INTRODUCTION

Educational establishments can also benefit from the Virtual Team Global Business Model. As mentioned in Chapter 1, students are often required to work in virtual teams to complete assignments as a group. They may be geographically dispersed and have to work with other students in locations across the country, and sometimes the world, to submit a joint assignment. Instructional designers (ISDs) are now creating curricula that integrate virtual team projects, and educators are encouraging the use of virtual team assignments for the following reasons:

- **Leadership**—It gives students an opportunity to lead a group and develop their project management skills. Some adult learners may already have management experience and know how to lead a group, but others need to develop their leadership skills, and virtual teams can provide them with opportunities to do this even if they have no desire to actually lead the team—for instance, if other adult learners are failing to participate.
- **Assessing and developing skills (patience, organization, time management, autonomy)**—It allows students' skills to be tested and developed. These include being patient when interacting with team members who have different work ethics, how to organize projects and allocate time to team and individual assignments, and how to exercise self-discipline and work autonomously.
- **Goal setting (accountability and deadlines)**—Educators are using virtual teams to develop students' abilities to set goals,

because they have to be accountable to their teammates and meet deadlines for assignment and grading purposes.

- **Project management (managing, guiding, setting timelines)**—It allows students to learn some of the intricacies of project management, including planning, organizing, and motivating one another in a group setting.
- **Collaborative learning (relinquishing personal agendas, fostering shared learning)**—Collaborative learning is one of the main reasons virtual teams are being integrated into higher education curricula, in the hope that students will hone their shared learning skills and learn to work cohesively in virtual teams, preparing them for future roles in the workforce.
- **Critical thinking (logical thought processes, problem solving)**—Higher education is a time to foster critical thinking skills. Hopefully, by working in groups, students can learn to approach problem solving logically, realizing that the team discussions and feedback are not personal, but constructive in producing high-quality assignments.

HOW DO VIRTUAL TEAMS WORK IN HIGHER EDUCATION?

As with businesses using the VTML, virtual teams in higher education (VTHEs) will not be effective unless management are active in initiating the virtual team tasks. Stakeholders, educators, and management need to be present and set protocols from the beginning of the project. Another point about using the VTML with higher education virtual teams is that usually a joint grade is provided for the whole assignment. Instructors may also reserve the right to grade individually, but they will need to review the dialogue and submissions meticulously to ensure fair grading. The VTML promotes this, since it demands that instructors maintain an active presence and check in regularly with teams.

In August 2012, 316 adult professionals were surveyed about virtual teams and asked the following question: "Do you think that students are comfortable working at a distance in virtual teams in the electronic classroom?" The results are shown in Table 6.1.

Table 6.1   Students' comfort on virtual teams

1. Yes	106	34%
2. No	210	66%
Totals	316	100%

If educators perceive that students are not comfortable working in virtual teams, improvement in this area should be high priority where virtual teamwork is integrated into the curriculum. An effective virtual team instructor sets students up for success, not failure, when working on team projects at a distance. Read the following message from a student:

> "I posted my virtual team assignment section for my team members to review, but also included a message to all of the team about my thoughts. I feel as if I am working independently. I refuse to allow this team to cause me to obtain a zero. This is the second teamwork assignment that has fallen completely on my shoulders because no one on the team cares about the grade. I'm not investing my money, effort, and time in this school to be wasted and fail because my team—that has been selected for me— doesn't want to participate. I care about my grades, and college is expensive. I have student loans to pay back, and want to ensure a bright future for my child—and not continually work dead end jobs. This teamwork is unfair. I am upset at this assignment and everyone's lack of participation."

This student has valid points. He has been appointed to this team to work toward a team grade, and team effort is lacking in the assignment. He has completed the majority of the work. His feelings of isolation are obvious, and his grade, the welfare of his child, his degree goals and money are all important to him—as they should be for any adult learners trying to continue their education. The instructor may have felt that the student was annoyed with him as well. This is clearly an impending conflict. Conflict in virtual teams occurs for a variety of reasons:

- The instructor may provide unclear or insufficient assignment instructions.
- Students may fail to read each others' messages.
- Miscommunication—students may not understand messages properly.
- Different work ethics—some students may work faster or slower than others; some may submit high-quality work, some low-quality work.
- Inconsistency—some students may fail to submit their assignment parts, or miss deadlines.
- There may be too few tasks to allocate within the assignment, resulting in a few members working more than others.

The list above can be categorized into four main reasons why conflict is prevalent in the online classroom when virtual teams are required and why the VTML can be helpful for higher education teams.

Preparation Conflict

Preparation conflict is usually the result of students' individual work ethics. Some students may be eager to get started on an assignment, while others may not check in or participate until after some decisions have been made by other team members on how to move forward. Some students may have read the assignment and decided on which part they want to complete while others may not yet have reviewed the instructions, let alone know what is expected or which part of the project they want to take on. Preparation conflict is similar to the situation described in Chapter 1 involving employees not understanding how to initiate the project and their responsibilities.

Preparation conflict can also result from students not understanding their assignments. Technical issues must be considered with team assignments as well. For example, a student on a virtual team may email his peers saying that he cannot open the file on the course materials page to review the instructions for the assignment. Remember, one of the precepts of the VTML is that projects are people-driven, not technology-driven. In this example, once the student is able to open the document and read the project instructions, he waits on his peers to explain what to do. He consistently relies on the team to carry the teamwork when faced with lack of clear guidance, instead of asking the instructor. Some students may have technical issues, may not understand any ambiguous instructions in the assignment, or may simply procrastinate about getting started.

Students may also comment that another student isn't participating. How long is it acceptable to wait before getting started on an assignment? What can instructors do to get them to participate? Although, as explained earlier when discussing personal work ethics, adults prefer to choose how they work, the VTML can help to provide guidance and set clear expectations. Finally, failure to coordinate in the initial stages means that two or more students may decide to take on the same part of an assignment, duplicating effort. The VTML process ensures accountability and clarifies responsibilities within the team.

Examples of potential preparation conflict
   "Professor, no one has checked in with my team, what should I do?"

   "Team, I've submitted my part of the assignment, but I haven't heard from anyone else."

   "Team, I don't understand this assignment and how we're going to divide it up."

   "Professor, I sent a message to the team that the assignment is due on Monday. It's already Friday, and nobody on the team has responded."

VTML preparation conflict solutions
The VTML promotes the resolution of preparation conflict in the following ways:

- It helps ISDs and instructors to provide clear instructions for the team assignment.
- It includes a process for assigning parts of the assignment to particular students.
- It avoids the duplication of submissions.
- It enables instructors to observe which students are active or inactive.
- It incorporates a Teamwork Skills Assessment.
- It sets clear rules and guidance to help students to understand expectations.

Students' observations

Student 1

"I believe virtual teams are needed and do add value to education. If virtual team assignments are balanced correctly and all students participate, the team works. I am just finishing a class that had a virtual team assignment every week, and was too much to manage with the individual assignments. In all honesty, I can see how students are not as active in teams, given the workload."

Student 2

"In some cases, virtual teams dwindle down, with two students remaining. One thing to consider is sometimes two heads are better than several that are not fully contributing. Depending on the strengths of each team member, sometimes fewer students can be rewarding on the team."

Student 3

"Virtual teams are one of the several reasons I will be transferring after I finish my associate program. I can see where they would help someone fresh out of high school and attending college courses having no previous work experience with teams. But I am an adult learner. I currently work in a team environment.

The difference being that I get paid to deal with the headaches that working on a team can bring. I would rather not come home and pay for the same headaches while earning my degree."

Student 4

"The team concept is very prevalent in business. People that I talk to with an MBA always comment on the team aspect of getting the MBA and the importance of teamwork. In the online environment, virtual teams attempt to mimic real teams. Anyone who is going to manage, teach, or work with people will have to learn how to work with in teams effectively. That is a reality."

Student 5

"Most universities are implementing some type of virtual team or collaboration among peers. There are numerous companies who don't participate in brainstorming sessions or business process meetings, so not every adult learner has the same opportunities to experience the team environment. The virtual team aspect is an adjustment to personalities similar to what we experience in the workplace. They do add value despite frustration that can be alleviated with more training on how to work at a distance with other students."

Leadership Conflict

Leaders within the team are responsible for compiling the assignment and seeing it through, setting deadlines and meeting times when everyone can be online together. Students may be reluctant to lead the group because they are unclear about the leader's roles and responsibilities. Conflict often arises when team members volunteer another student who is an active participant to a leadership role, leaving him or her to carry out the bulk of the work. Some adult learners are more assertive, and as leaders of the team, they may be not receptive to other members' contributions, again leading to conflict. Some virtual team leaders may be so dominant that they edit others team members' work because it doesn't meet their personal work quality specifications, and this can also cause conflict. Finally, some leaders may only request help from teammates they see as responsible or who are personal favorites, and this can lead to jealousy and resentment among other team members.

Examples of potential sources of leadership conflict
> *"I have to compile the assignment because no one else has volunteered."*

> *"I guess that I am the team leader again this week."*

> *"Here's what Scott should have submitted; Scott didn't follow the professor's instructions."*

> *"I'm going to complete this project myself because I don't like what has been submitted to the team."*

VTML leadership conflict solutions
The VTML promotes the resolution of leadership conflict in the following ways:

- It provides check-points for team leaders to gauge effective control of the team.
- It encourages active involvement through meetings and the exchange of messages to balance participation.
- It clarifies the leader's role on VTHEs.
- It allows instructors to grade and critique students' team participation.

Student Participation Conflict

Students' failure to participate results in a huge area of team conflict, as expressed in the student's concerns quoted at the beginning of this chapter. These issues are also addressed effectively by the VTML. If team members are inactive online and go missing from online classes for weeks at a time, what happens to the virtual team assignment? It usually means that one or a few members have to complete the assignment for the whole team. Student participation issues can stem from the fact that some virtual team members are slackers. Some may not be fully engaged in the team assignment, but may still be submitting their individual class assignments. If team members submit partially completed work to the team and others have to finish it off for them, this can lead to student participation conflict, not least because some may resent the fact that underperformers may receive the same team grade as them despite their minimal contributions.

Student participation conflict can also arise when active VTMs think that the instructor hasn't noticed that inactive students are not participating. The students on the team who are working may start to post messages complaining about those who aren't contributing and the unfair grading inequality that may ensue. On one team, the instructor hadn't been checking in, a slacker student received the same grading as his teammates, and then posted his grade on the team forum (an inappropriate action in itself), leading to great resentment.

Examples of potential sources of student participation conflict
> *"Professor, Tina was on our team for the first two weeks, is she still in class?"*

> *"Team, I noticed Tina's participating in the main forum in class but not in the team area."*

> *"Team, I agree with what others have submitted, though I haven't submitted anything myself."*

> *"Professor, have you noticed what's occurring on the team? Only a few of us are doing all the work."*

VTML student participation conflict solutions
The VTML promotes the resolution of student participation conflict in the following ways:

• It enables instructors to grade their students' virtual team assignments more accurately.

- It gives students clear guidance about specific assignment tasks, increasing the quality of the deliverables.
- It reveals which students need help and which are slacking on the virtual team.
- It alleviates students' concerns that their grades will be affected by slackers.

Students' observations

Student 1

"Virtual teams are a part of the 'real world,' depending on your goals. If you intend to manage, make decisions, motivate others, work in a team, establish guidelines, procedures and protocols, facilitate meetings, collaborate with others on anything, then these experiences, no matter how horrible they may seem at times, are relevant to your future in the business arena."

Student 2

"I am a better manager, more patient and understanding, and still conduct disciplinary proceedings when necessary, because of my team experiences. I was recently told by a coworker that I am more approachable, and I attribute this to the hardships associated with the virtual team approach."

Student 3

"I was not always agreeable to virtual teams. I was angry about not having an option to work in teams. After several team projects, I learned ways to cope and manage teams."

Student 4

"I am not saying it is right that there are students who do not have the same zest for education as others, and fail to meet expectations. However, I am saying, this is real life! We will run across coworkers, partners, and team members who are only working for the paycheck and do not have the same zest for their job or project as we do; yet because they are in attendance and meet 'corporate' expectations, we must work with them and find

*ways to get the most out of our collaboration; it makes sense to
start in college."*

Student 5

*"It is our choice to take on these academic studies despite
other responsibilities. We must make the best of this choice and
try to work in teams effectively, although strong guidance from
instructors and the school helps."*

Instructor Presence Conflict

Instructor presence is a concern on some virtual teams. If the instructor doesn't conduct evaluations or check in with the team to assess the dialogue and student contributions, this can lead to conflict. If students don't feel that the instructor is concerned about the flow of the team, they may devote little or no effort to completing the team assignment. Students comment that the lack of instructor presence to help with team fluidity is problematic and discouraging. As pointed out earlier, some students may feel that others are receiving grades based on their work alone, and not their contributions to the virtual team, or that the team's overall grade is being dragged down by slackers. In addition, constant bickering and snide messages between students that may result will go unaddressed if the instructor isn't active, leading to students feeling marginalized in the online classroom. The absence of team evaluations and open, formal ways to reassure students that they are being graded fairly is an aspect of instructor presence that can lead to grave conflict.

Examples of potential sources of instructor presence conflict

 *"The instructor, didn't bother reading my submission last week, so
as long as we submit something from the team, it doesn't matter."*

 *"Team, I'm going to credit all our names on this assignment
except Bill, because he didn't contribute, and I refuse to let him
obtain a grade for my work."*

"Professor, with all due respect, I'm burnt out this week. Last week was no better. Only a few of us are active, and I hope you're reading our messages so that certain members won't end up obtaining a grade for contributing when they didn't."

"Professor, have you been reading the messages on the team forum? Two members are being very disrespectful, and the rude comments are escalating."

VTML instructor presence conflict solutions

The VTML promotes the resolution of instructor presence conflict in the following ways:

- It ensures that instructors are accountable for facilitating the team assignment.
- It incorporates open evaluation to ensure that students are being graded fairly.
- It encourages instructor presence through check-in and monitoring.

The VTML in higher education relies on active instructor presence. As highlighted in Chapter 4, Joseph Grenny, co-author of the *New York Times* best-seller *Crucial Conversations*, explained that when team members encounter challenges, they may either resort to silence or other passive coping strategies, or they may become verbally violent or attacking toward other team members.[1] Students posting messages to other students out of frustration in virtual teams with a lack of instructor presence is problematic for both the team and the reputation of the educational establishment.

Students' observations

Student 1

"I am turning to the chat room for help. Peers, I'm on a virtual team right now and there are five members. Unfortunately, only

---

1   Kerry Patterson, Joseph Grenny, Ron McMillan, and Al Switzler (2012), *Crucial Conversations: Tools for Talking When Stakes are High*, 2nd edn., New York: McGraw-Hill.

two of us are willing to do ANY work. I know I'm not the only one who has experienced this .... *My teacher, sadly, doesn't require team evaluations, so the only way to let her know and try to get some reprieve from all this extra work would be to rat out my teammates."*

Student 2

"I'm a few classes away from graduation with a very high GPA, and I have been dealing with virtual team issues since the first class. Being a leader of the team has helped. I carried a lot of my teamwork."

Student 3

"I don't agree with the requirement and the grading weight for the virtual team assignments, I understand that they are required and help us learn to work with others, but do they? I find myself frustrated most of the time. I think that they should be optional, not obligatory."

Student 4

"I am not ranting about virtual teams, but teachers need to hold these students accountable—bottom line! I am extremely annoyed with my virtual teams.

Student 5

"I think virtual teams are a big joke. On the first assignment where we have to assess our strengths, students promise to be on time with their work, communicate, work hard, and be perfect team players. Reality is different. You know who works and who doesn't without any accountability."

USING THE VTML IN HIGHER EDUCATION

Online courses are usually not designed by the instructors who will be delivering them. Some instructors do design their own courses, but many are drawn up by instructional designers (ISDs), who review the learning objectives for the course, the course textbook, and supplementary material to establish the appropriate design. ISDs are classified as management in the VTML, since they are the course initiators. ISDs are responsible for providing students with material to work with and viable team assignments to ensure that virtual teamwork is effective in the classroom.

In order to set goals, objectives, and tasks for an assignment, the ISD must review the purpose of the course. In doing so, the ISD can follow the guidance laid out by the VTML. When designing the syllabus, the ISD must ensure that sufficient points are allocated for the virtual team assignment on the grading scale (an example can be found later this chapter). This is one way to ensure that students will participate in the team with the same dedication they devote to completing individual assignments.

When designing a course using the VTML as a distance teamwork model, ISDs will set goals, objectives, and tasks, and are also responsible for allocating the due dates for assignments.

For example, if the ISD is designing an "Introduction to Education" course using virtual teams, he or she may set the following goals and objectives.

Goals:

- Students will understand the principles of education.
- Students will assess their study skills and enhance their study strategies.
- Students will develop interpersonal skills to help facilitate educational discussions.
- Students will enhance their academic writing skills.

In the VTML, the objectives follow the goals:

Goal 1: Students will understand the principles of education.
Objective 1: Develop an understanding of basic andragogy principles.
Objective 2: Demonstrate learning styles and learning theories.

Goal 2: Students will assess their study skills and enhance their study strategies.
Objective 1: Describe note-taking and reading methods.
Objective 2: Understand time management principles and motivation types.
Goal 3: Students will develop interpersonal skills to help facilitate educational discussions.
Objective 1: Recognize the structure of small group discussion communication.
Objective 2: Demonstrate the basic communication e-model.
Goal 4: Students will enhance their academic writing skills.
Objective 1: Summarize the requirements for the essential skills of writing and research to achieve academic success.
Objective 2: Describe the need to develop critical thinking skills for success in university studies.

Now that the ISD has set the goals and objectives, he or she can design the tasks involved for each objective.

Note: The difference between applying the VTML to higher education virtual teams as opposed to those in business is that the ISD will actually design the assignments that equate to the tasks for each objective.

Since virtual team assignments are integrated into curricula, not every student assignment will be a group one—some will be individual assignments. Group assignments involving virtual teams usually begin in week two or sometimes week four of a course, depending on its length. The initial weeks are usually devoted to familiarizing students with the course and its objectives. Applying the VTML, here is an example of individual and virtual team assignments created by an ISD:

Goal 1: Students will understand the principles of education.
Objective 1: Develop an understanding of basic andragogy principles.
Individual Task 1: Explain andragogy principles (discussion assignment).
Virtual Team Task 2: Create an outline with points explaining andragogy (definitions of terms associated with the model,

characteristics of andragogy, examples of the model, critiques of the model).

Objective 2: Demonstrate learning styles and learning theories.

Individual Task 1: Complete the Learning Style Assessment.

Virtual Team Task 2: Compare and contrast four of the learning theories (essay).

Goal 2: Students will assess their study skills and enhance their study strategies.

Objective 1: Describe note-taking and reading methods.

Individual Task 1: Provide an application of reading methods (Word document).

Virtual Team Task 2: Complete the note-taking assignment using different note-taking styles—Cornell, Outline, Charting, Clustering (chart).

Objective 2: Understand time management principles and motivation types.

Task 1: Complete the Time Management Assessment (quiz).

Task 2: Create the Time Management Calendar (Word document)

Virtual Team Task 3: Explain motivation types (intrinsic and extrinsic), and provide four applications of both motivations (Word document).

Goal 3: Students will develop interpersonal skills to help facilitate educational discussions.

Objective 1: Recognize the structure of small group discussion communication.

Individual Tasks 1: Complete the Interpersonal Communication Quiz.

Virtual Team Task 2: Create small group dyads based on the following topics: self-concept, active listening, written correspondences, and perception (Word document).

Objective 2: Demonstrate the Basic Communication e-Model.

Individual Task 1: Complete the Communication e-Model Assignment (flowchart)

Individual Task 2: Respond to the e-Model prompts (discussion questions).

Goal 4: Students will enhance their academic writing skills.

Objective 1: Summarize the requirements for the essential skills of writing and research to achieve academic success.

Individual Task 1: Complete the writing and research process assignment (Word document).

Virtual Team Task 2: Write an eight-page essay including the following sections: "Background of Andragogy Principles," "Arguments about Andragogy Principles," "Andragogy and Technology," "The Future of Andragogy for Educators."

Objective 2: Describe the need to develop critical thinking skills for success in university studies.

Virtual Team Task 1: Generate discussions about critical thinking and college success for first-term students (discussion in team forum).

Virtual Team Task 2: Select the four main points discussed and submit a one-page summary of each based on the discussions (Word document).

Assignments

Team assignments must be viable, and they should include multiple parts, as in the "Introduction to Education" course examples, so that each VTM has a part to complete. Here are some ideas for assignments that involve multiple parts and are ideal for virtual teams:

- **PowerPoint presentations**—keep slides to minimum, such as three to five for each member, and no more than 15–20 slides.
- **Business or any other types of proposals**—including a marketing section, an executive summary, financial items such as a cost analysis, and so on.
- **Needs assessments**—provide a problem or performance gap that is workforce-based relating to the subject of the course and have students analyze the issue and compose resolutions.
- **Internet research**—this is a good learning team project, which could involve students conducting "scavenger hunts," searching for peer-reviewed articles, gathering interesting observations about a topic, then reporting their findings as a team on one topic offering diverse perspectives.
- **Training modules**—each student could write a section of a training module, develop a workshop or course, or draw up objectives, discussion questions, and group activities for each

section to illustrate their knowledge on a topic of their choice or as if they were facilitating a workshop, and so on.

- **Case studies**—create or search for factual case studies and scenarios to use as group projects, and create resolution strategies.

The ISD needs to design projects so they can be divided into parts to allocate to individual team members. A suitable team assignment will include sufficient detail and parts to allow both instructors and students to meet their responsibilities in terms of fairness and quality when working at a distance.

The following pages offer some ideas for virtual team projects in several subject areas. Notice how each part is allocated to an individual team member. In designing a course, ISDs (or instructors, if they are designing the course themselves) can follow this strategy when creating tasks so that when the instructor is facilitating the virtual team, it is clear which student is responsible for completing which part of the assignment. The ISD or instructor can allocate parts to individual students, or the students themselves can be invited to choose which part of the assignment they want to complete. This will be discussed in more detail later.

MARKETING COURSES

Here is a suggested assignment to design a Marketing Plan for Smith Builders home improvement store using print advertising:

Team Member 1: Marketing Strategy—Compose a list of product offerings, a mission statement for the company, and marketing objectives.

Team Member 2: Marketing Overview—Provide details about advertising for existing stores, grand openings of stores, and how many pre-printed advertisements will go to stores.

Team Member 3: Marketing Plan—Decide in which newspapers and magazines insert advertisements will run, and based on the marketing overview, decide which homes or neighborhoods the mailings will go to, and how many radio advertisements and media outlets will be used.

Team Member 4: Cost and Quantity Summary—For the selected newspapers, decide how many inserts will go in them based on the Marketing Plan, find out what it will cost to print these inserts based on each newspaper's rates, and compose a cost summary chart.

Team Member 5: Marketing Summary—based on each element demographics, pre-prints, newspapers used, what are the marketing recommendations for both established stores and those that will have grand openings with regard to print advertising and other media.

Additional Information

The ISD should know beforehand how many student have enrolled on the course, and should provide additional information so that instructors have resources available to use as extra assignment sections in the event that further students join it, as well as contingencies if students drop out. Additional parts for the marketing assignment could include the following:

- **A product summary**—add specific types of products to advertise.
- **A demographics section**—identify zip or postal codes, ethnicities, home owners to target for marketing.
- **Graphics or pictures**—illustrate products featured in marketing plan.
- **A flow chart**—set out the overall proposed marketing plan.

If the instructor has not designed the course, he or she may not be authorized to edit it, in which case it will be necessary to adapt what has been provided by the ISD to tailor it to a particular virtual team. However, it may be acceptable to provide some ideas for additional sections as described above, depending on the syllabus. The important point is that the ISD or whoever designs the course needs to ensure that the virtual team assignment is suitable for the number of students expected to participate and the instructor who will be expected to mediate conflict and facilitate the team.

MEDICAL COURSES

Case Studies

Case studies are effective in medical course virtual team assignments, allowing students to apply what they are learning and to compare their answers with others in the virtual team. Here are some suggestions for case studies:

> **Team Member 1:** A 23-year-old man presents with a three-month history of unexplained fever. He also suffers from asthma and severe back pain. What is the diagnosis?
>
> **Team Member 2:** A 61-year-old woman presents with progressive shortness of breath, pain in her side, fever, and weakness. A pinkish rash is observable on her extremities. What is the diagnosis?
>
> **Team Member 3:** A 57-year-old woman presents with a four-month history of gastric pain with nausea and vomiting. She has previously been diagnosed with lymphoma. What is the diagnosis?
>
> **Team Member 4:** An 80-year-old man presents with hiccups, dizziness, and nausea. What is the diagnosis?

Charts

Another effective method is to use charts.

Provide a basic chart using Microsoft Excel or Microsoft Word, and ask the students to draw up at least five components for any topic. This example concerns a healthy diet:

> Ask each team member to select a health screening test, then describe that test in full based on the following:

- Describe the factors that aid those with cardiovascular issues.
- Create a model of a healthy diet.

ISDs should take into account students' abilities with graphics or Excel charts or spreadsheets, and avoid making them too complicated, especially for an introductory course, and in particular when designing assignments for basic learners. Simpler team assignments are sometimes more effective in developing skills regarding learning outcomes and collaborative work at a distance.

INFORMATION TECHNOLOGY COURSES

Technological Advances

There have been a number of advances and changes in usage of software and hardware over recent years. Ask students to select a few and discuss their selections in a cohesive document comparing the situation five or ten years ago and how they have developed. Here are some ideas for topics:

- USB memory sticks
- netbooks
- smart phones
- tablet computers
- fax machines
- printers.

The assignment could consist of the following:

Team Member 1: Explain the past usage of item one selected by your team.
Team Member 2: Explain the past usage of item two selected your team.
Team Member 3: Explain current usage and innovations regarding item one selected by your team.

Team Member 4: Explain current usage and innovations regarding item two selected by your team.

Social Media

Social media is a huge topic. Students can explore the different platforms available, issues of security, privacy, and new forms of communication, and assess the communication models of social media platforms such as Facebook, LinkedIn, Twitter, or YouTube.

E-commerce

E-commerce is a great project for teamwork, and allows for creativity among students.

Online transactions offer retailers such as Sports Authority, Home Depot, or Best Buy opportunities to attract new business and additional options for selling their products. Ask the team to explore the advantages and disadvantages of comparing costs, products, and availability online as opposed to going into a bricks-and-mortar store.

Another option is to ask the team to help a fictitious CEO in charge of a hotel chain to set up an e-commerce system, drawing on the O-Span Youth example described in earlier chapters for guidance:

> The CEO wants to start a new hotel chain. He wants to advertise its comfortable rooms, Internet access, Continental breakfasts, and the ability to make reservations by phone or via the website, allowing negotiation about the rates.
>
> Ask each virtual team member to choose a part of the assignment and assist the CEO in designing this e-commerce project, then create a PowerPoint presentation that summarizes the team's solutions.

Additional Information

As well as providing additional information to the online instructor, offering the instructor other options if there are not enough parts of an assignment is a good idea. For example, the e-commerce assignment is well suited to dividing the team into four subgroups rather than allocating parts to individuals. The ISD should provide the information and options to the instructor during Communication Phase 1.

EDUCATION COURSES

Students in this field may want to teach, or may be interested in a career in educational leadership.

Teaching

Ask the team to create a course or elements of a course each week:

Team Member 1: Course Descriptions—Design a syllabus component and a course module.
Team Member 2: Learning Objectives—Design a syllabus component and a course module.
Team Member 3: Grading Scales—Design a syllabus component and a course module.
Team Member 4: Assignment Due Dates—Design a syllabus component and a course module.

Each module should be based on the overall learning objectives that have been established, and students can be asked to devise discussion questions, assignments, and tests for each of them. ISDs should ensure that the assignments are engaging, allow for learning, and are team-oriented.

Leadership Skills

Educational leadership courses are another instance where utilize case studies can be useful, providing students with opportunities to develop their problem solving skills and apply conflict management techniques. One option is to ask the team to try to obtain funding and grants for a fictitious school, documenting the processes and research involved.

Once again, the ISD will have to assess the learning outcomes for the course to create viable virtual teams, and this also applies to individual assignments.

Composition

Essays are fine if everyone in the team contributes, and allocating students an essay topic that allows them to practice a particular persuasive strategy will help them to develop dialogue in their team.

Provide a list of topics and ask each team member to select one for their essay, preferably on a current issue to excite their interest. For example:

- Should marijuana be legal for medicinal purposes?
- Does disadvantage among children lead to high crime rates among adults?
- Are Americans' privacy rights at risk?
- Will the drug wars ever be reduced, or is it a money making business that is here to stay?

You could divide the persuasive strategies as follows:

Team Member 1: Apply the sympathetic persuasive strategy to your selected topic.
Team Member 2: Apply the assertive persuasive strategy to your selected topic.
Team Member 3: Apply the propaganda persuasive strategy to your selected topic.
Team Member 4: Apply the fear persuasive strategy to your selected topic.

Grammar

Another option is to ask the students to explore grammar rules.

Ask them to explain grammar rules such as the usage of semicolons, commas, or apostrophes, and to recap the rules in five to ten original sentences that demonstrate the correct usage. It is important to ensure that the sentences are original and that the examples have not been copied from the Internet, for instance. Plagiarism detection software is useful for English courses.

A good English assignment will cover grammar rules, pre-writing activities, and tailoring writing to a particular audience (for example, managerial, lay, or expert), introducing different types of essays and asking students not only to write essays, but to explain their views on the parts of speech and the writing and research process—this can be accomplished collaboratively.

PSYCHOLOGY COURSES

Psychology is a vast field full of interesting topics. Mental and personality disorders are among the topics students can research while working as virtual teams, providing treatment options. It is particularly important for ISDs to bear in mind the learning outcomes for the course in designing the team assignments, posing self-questions or contacting subject matter experts to help in the process.

For example, one of the learning outcomes for a psychology course could be to identify issues associated with psychopaths. A person with a psychopathic personality shows signs of antisocial behavior and lack of ability to love, or issues with establishing close personal relationships. The parts of the assignment could be allocated as follows:

Team Member 1: Research and discuss the antisocial behavior of a psychopath.

Team Member 2: Research and discuss the psychopath's lack of ability to establish close personal relationships.

Team Member 3: Research and discuss the psychopath's work environment challenges.

Team Member 4: Research and discuss the consequences of the psychopath's behavior in society/community groups.

The students could also be asked to discuss particular mental or personality disorders as a group, describing their characteristics, then recommending treatment options.

* * *

All this might seem like hard work and a lot of information to provide, but the goal is to provide high-quality assignments incorporating sufficient substantive parts to enable all members of the virtual team to participate. ISDs should create assignments that can be divided into at least five parts, if necessary. The additional information should provide instructors with indications of the ideal team size and ideas about ways to facilitate the team.

COMMUNICATION PHASE 1

In higher education, during Communication Phase 1, ISDs meet with instructors to discuss the assignments and expectations. This should be a synchronous meeting or webinar if the ISD is meeting with several instructors to review the course design. Once again, following the VTML helps keep all parties up to date, and instructors should have access to the course materials at this point to familiarize themselves with the course design. Sometimes instructors don't gain access to the course materials until a week before the course begins, allowing limited time in which it's only possible to read through the syllabus, so they have to learn about the course as they go along. It is advisable to provide the instructor with access to the course materials, or at least the curriculum, a month ahead of time to allow for preparation, especially in the case of new courses.

During Communication Phase 1, the ISD reviews the goals, objectives, assignment tasks, and any special instructions. Since the deliverables are the assignments and these have been set up by the ISD, instructors do not need to convert tasks into deliverables, but they do have to conduct the Virtual Team Skills Assessment and complete the other tasks that will be explained later in this chapter. During this phase, the ISD provides a review of the course in the form of an ISD Report.

ISD Report

The ISD Report is the equivalent of the Virtual Team Project Form that business managers present during Communication Phase 1. The ISD Report sets out the goals, objectives, and assignments, and the ISD previews this during the meeting so that the instructor is aware of how the course will flow, and can then refer to a written record of it during student team assignments, along with the syllabus.

ISD Report example
Goals:
Goal 1: Students will understand the principles of education.
Goal 2: Students will assess their study skills and enhance their study strategies.
Goal 3: Students will develop interpersonal skills to help facilitate educational discussions.
Goal 4: Students will enhance their academic writing skills.
Assignments:
Individual Task 1: Explain the principles of andragogy.
Virtual Team Task 2: Create a point-by-point outline explaining andragogy.
Individual Task 1: Complete the Learning Style Assessment.
Virtual Team Task 2: Compare and contrast learning theories.
Individual Task 1: Provide an application of reading methods (Word document).
Virtual Team Task 2: Complete a note-taking assignment using different note-taking styles (Cornell, Outline, Charting, Clustering).
Additional Information: Week five features two virtual team assignments, so please plan accordingly with the student leaders.

Educators need to take systematic steps and actions to make virtual teams effective and flow smoothly. Too often, virtual teams are not effective, and students shy away from establishments that offer them as part of their curricula because of their poor reputation and the lack of active management from educators. When virtual teams are well organized, students feel comfortable and the reputation of virtual teamwork is enhanced. Applying the VTML helps in this regard.

The Instructor as Project Manager

Now that the instructor is aware of the assignments that he or she will have in the course, individual and group assignments, he or she is now ready to complete the tasks set out in the VTML. As stated above, instructors serve as project managers the VTML. Although, this role need never be explicitly explained to the students, the functions should be completed. Essential tasks the instructor needs to complete using the VTML as a guide include the following:

- Ask students to complete the VTML Skills Assessment and evaluate it.
- Assign students to teams and allocate deliverables (assigning a deliverable to a specific student is optional).
- Assign the team leader—this person will serve as the virtual team guide.
- Check in consistently with the team.

Let's review each of these points in detail.

Virtual Team Skills Assessment

The Virtual Team Skills Assessment Form described in Chapter 3 can be adapted for students in higher education virtual teams, along with same evaluation of results. The main difference is the roles that students often display on virtual teams. Although accountability is built into the VTML, instructors still have to bear in mind that some roles that are not healthy for virtual team progress may emerge among the students. Students exhibiting the "I'll do it" role may become exhausted trying to do the work others won't complete, such as any students in the "slacker" role, who may do only limited or no work to advance the team assignment. Students exhibiting the "passive" role may not volunteer to complete any parts of the assignment, although they may not necessarily be unwilling to do so if asked. Students exhibiting the "assertive" role may be demanding and like to work autonomously, taking on the majority of the assignment work and avoiding team collaboration, or bossing about other team members.

What is important is that *instructors grade accordingly* for participation when roles emerge that do not foster teamwork and result in high-quality contributions. Instructors have to check in regularly with the team and VTG to identify any team issues. Getting students to work to resolve any issues in team forums is an ideal way to keep track of all this. Another strategy is to assign students parts of assignments to complete. This can help to avoid issues, but there is also value in allowing students the freedom to select their own parts of assignments.

Assign teams and deliverables
Instructors are responsible for assigning students to teams, but once they have done so, they don't necessarily have to assign specific students to specific assignment parts. As stated above, once the ISD has designed the course and instructors are familiar with the course structure and the class roster, allowing students to decide which part of an assignment they will be responsible for completing provides them with options to work on what they feel comfortable completing, depending on the subject. If students choose their own assignment parts, the instructor is ultimately responsible for documenting this. The VTG can convey them to the instructor during weekly assignment updates. If the establishment uses a software management system (such as Pearson LearningStudio or Blackboard Learning System) for administration, each student can post a message on a thread in the team forum identifying the part of the assignment he or she will complete. In such systems, instructors have access to the class roster, from which they can assign students to teams, usually by clicking on the students' names and dragging them to the appropriate team area. Table 6.2 shows an example of team assignment.

Table 6.2   Higher education virtual team assignment example

Team A	Team B	Team C	Team D
Daren	Harry	Fin	Reah
Janis	Aline	Julie	Alex
Paul	Pristine	Laura	Blane
Lisa	Zoren	Simon	Marcus

Some instructors compile virtual teams according to time zone: for example, Eastern Standard Time students on one team and Central Time students on another team, and so forth. Unless the student is in a location where there is a large difference in time zones from other team members, this may not matter as much as ensuring that students allocate sufficient time to do the work. Also, since the VTML encourages forming teams according to members' skills, it can be more important to use the Virtual Team Skills Assessment to ensure that the make-up of teams will help to bring assignments to fruition.

Having assigned the students to teams, the instructor can then either allocate tasks to individual students, or allow them to select their own.

Here's an example of the distribution of tasks for a particular assignment:

Virtual team task: Create a point-by-point learning outline based on the andragogy model.
- Daren: Define the terms associated with andragogy.
- Janis: Describe the characteristics of andragogy.
- Paul: Provide examples of the model.
- Lisa: Provide a critique of the model.

COMMUNICATION PHASE 2

We now enter Communication Phase 2.

Assign the team leader (VTG)

The instructor can now assign a student VTG for each team assignment. If the school doesn't have its own facility for conducting conference calls, the instructor can use a resource such as FreeConferenceCall. This provides an opportunity for the instructor to explain how the virtual team will flow, clarify the role of the VTG and introduce him or her to the team, and discuss the skills assessment and the allocation of parts of the assignment, as well the importance of participating and completing the assigned or chosen parts and communicating with other team members. It is important to provide a clear explanation of virtual teamwork and the expectations. Some students may never have worked in virtual teams before, so this is an essential aspect of Communication Phase 2.

A different student can take on the role of VTG for each assignment, or depending on the length of the course, it may be necessary for the same student to serve as VTG for two or more assignments. The VTG will facilitate the assignments and meetings, but may need to ask the instructor for assistance if the team is not flowing well, although if the initial stages have been carried out correctly, conflict should be minimal.

Consistent check-in

Instructors should check in consistently with their virtual teams. The ISD should have defined a grading scale that includes a participation element (see Table 6.3 for an example). Instructors should offer observations about participation during virtual team feedback sessions, and provide progress notes to the students as part of the weekly grading.

Table 6.3   Grading percentage breakdown

Discussions	20%
Quizzes	10%
Individual assignment part	40%
Team assignment	30%
Total	**100%**

If there are noticeable issues among the team, it may be necessary to provide the students with a more detailed breakdown of the participation assessment. The 30 percent allocated to the team assignment can be broken down as follows:

> 10 percent—The student has checked in consistently (at least three times a week) and participated actively to help create a collaborative team environment.
>
> 15 percent—The student submitted the allocated assignment part, and it was satisfactory.
>
> 5 percent—The student has approved the final draft.

Notice that a percentage is allocated for approving the final draft. This is because every team member must be active during the final review of the project, approving it, and demonstrating that a concerted effort was made to edit and review the submission to ensure its quality.

The VTG (Student Role)

The VTG is responsible for setting up any online meetings for the team and gathering the assignment parts. Because students take on this role in the VTHE, instructors will need to be careful to check in consistently with their teams to ensure that the VTGs are not abusing their power or alienating their peers, or on the other hand, that they are not overwhelmed by their role. Instructors should also make clear to students that they will check in regularly and be available if conflict occurs. Since some ISDs are contractors and don't work full-time for the establishment, it is particularly important for ISDs and instructors to meet in the initial stages of course design, but further meetings during the rest of the course shouldn't be necessary unless there are problems or questions about the assignments.

A student VTG has fewer responsibilities than a business VTG. The student VTG keeps the instructor updated on team progress and makes sure that assignments are submitted by the due dates by coordinating and collecting each member's work, but is not responsible for imposing discipline to ensure that team members complete the tasks they have been allocated.

After all team members have submitted their parts of the assignment, the VTG may compile them into one coherent document, then submit the assignment to the appropriate online area for the instructor to grade it. The VTG should not edit other students' submissions. Each student should be responsible for the quality of his or her own work. The VTG can preview and ensure that all elements of the assignment are present, but if there are issues with the quality of work students have submitted or they have failed to complete their part of the assignment, it is the instructor's responsibility to intervene and/or grade accordingly.

VTMs (Students)

Students working at a distance are virtual team members as defined by the VTML. Communication Phase 2 will convey to them what they are expected to do for their assignment tasks and the role of the VTG. They will be aware that their instructor will check in regularly to assess their participation and the quality of their work. They will understand that they are not alone, and will be clear about the due dates and the expectations of their deliverables. Now they are ready for Communication Phase 3.

COMMUNICATION PHASE 3

In Communication Phase 3, the VTG for each assignment should keep the instructor informed about any concerns. If any team members are inactive despite the guidance provided by the VTML, instructors should be aware of the reasons behind this because they are checking in regularly, and should grade accordingly. Students' life events may be impeding their participation, or they may just be exhibiting the "slacker" role. If team members have to complete other students' tasks along with their own to enable the whole assignment to be completed, here are some considerations:

- The instructor should ensure that a student who has completed an additional or incomplete part of an assignment doesn't have to do so for the following assignment. This means that the VTG or another student may have to complete the task, but the instructor should explain that the protocol is that team responsibilities should rotate, as in the case of the VTG.
- If the VTG is unable to take on any additional tasks, another student will need to volunteer. The instructor should explain the proxy system to team members.
- If several team members are missing and the assignment is in jeopardy, the instructor may have to restructure the requirements to allow those students who did participate to receive credit for their work without having complete the entire assignment. This is the worst-case scenario, but it needs to be an option when dealing with students working at a distance.

The instructor may choose to conduct an informal review of the draft submission and offer feedback to the students so they can improve it. This could take the form of a synchronous meeting, perhaps using instant messaging, in which case a copy of the draft should be distributed for discussion. Alternatively, the instructor can review the assignment on his or her own before it is due and provide the VTG with any suggestions for edits to pass along to students. Informal meetings give instructors opportunities to check in with VTGs and provide general feedback to support them in their role.

The instructor is always responsible for conducting the final review and grading assignments. Any specific grade critiques should always be conveyed in private, and the instructor should never discuss other students' grades with the VTG.

At the end of Communication Phase 3, the students will be ready to submit their work.

ONLINE INSTRUCTORS' OBSERVATIONS ABOUT THE BENEFITS OF WORKING IN VIRTUAL TEAMS

"When a virtual team works well, students get excited about it and it is great fun to see them get involved in the work."

"For professionals this is great, but I teach for another school where virtual teams are part of every course. Students struggle with this in their first and second year of college. By the time they are seniors most do well."

"The virtual team approach allows for learners to share their experience, which impacts learning."

"The main benefit of having students work in virtual teams is the preparation it gives them for the process, which is prevalent in the professional realm. Virtual teams in a professional context help to maximize efficiency and enable project participants to proceed with planning/development, even deployment, regardless of physical location. Virtual collaboration also saves a company travel costs."

"Virtual teamwork is always beneficial professionally. If professionals are working on a project, teamwork will make it more effective. I do not think that all students benefit from teamwork. Too often, one or two students do all the work."

"Virtual teams may encourage a bit more engagement with the subject matter and make some individuals feel less isolated."

"Yes, students can learn how to work successfully with others to complete a project at a distance. This is important, because in most careers students will have to rely on teammates to complete a project."

"The benefits are that information is shared and people learn through collaboration. Also, people who share the same goals (instructors teaching the same courses) can meet and share information in a virtual team when there is no reasonable way to bring them together to meet and collaborate face-to-face."

"The collaboration aspect is great for professionals and students who understand the importance of virtual team work. It can be beneficial to learn from others' perspectives. Online learning offers a chance for students to learn from others across the globe!"

"Students will have to work with others in a job setting. I think virtual teams help to prepare them for working in groups. They also have to learn what to do when someone doesn't pull their weight in a team. I think it is a valuable experience."

"Virtual teams provide flexibility and availability for students and professionals. A number of students would not be able to attend traditional brick-and-mortar schools because of location, family and/or work issues, etc. The virtual team setup opens up a number of opportunities for them—for professionals, virtual teams broader their base of connections with other professionals."

"Virtual teams are applicable to real life."

"The primary benefit is the sharing of knowledge. In a traditional team meeting, words are lost or overlooked during the process of the meeting. In a virtual meeting, all information is recorded and able to be addressed asynchronously. More information is shared in virtual teams."

"The exchange of ideas thanks to multiple perspectives is the result of working with teams at a distance."

"Any time there is an opportunity to bring together different viewpoints, it's important to do so. A team can solve complex problems or issues that might prove too daunting for an individual. Being able to connect with people from diverse backgrounds and in distant locations without the expense of travel is a valuable tool, especially in this economy."

ONLINE INSTRUCTORS' OBSERVATIONS ABOUT THE CHALLENGES OF WORKING IN VIRTUAL TEAMS

"When a team doesn't work well, good students get frustrated and less motivated students will try to get by on the work of others. Although they can't really succeed at this, the perceived unfairness of it upsets some students. These aren't problems that only virtual teams have—they plague all teamwork."

"Waiting for responses from others, miscommunication, lack of full participation by all team members—most are extremely frustrated by the process and see no benefit at all."

"One or two people do all the work on some virtual teams, or leaders are chosen who don't lead well."

"From my experience teaching classes with virtual teamwork, the biggest challenge is that students wait too long to contribute to the team or do not contribute at all."

"I have never been on a virtual team where everyone pitched in. Usually about one third of the people actually participate, and the rest of the members do not do any of the work, or even show up, for the most part."

"Virtual teamwork challenges involve mostly getting the students to participate, take the lead, and set an assignment plan."

"Of course, some students won't participate like they should, but that's true of any assignment."

"Students are unfamiliar and insecure working in virtual teams; they need instruction and guidance not only with the tasks the team must complete, but how to negotiate among themselves."

"Getting a project done in a timely manner presents virtual team frustration. Some members wait till the last minute to participate, which slows processes down. It takes motivation of the highest order to get a team to participate to the maximum at a distance."

"Many of the students do not do their part. Some do not do anything, and expect someone else to do all of the work. Some are upset because they have to come in earlier in the week to class than normal to participate in the virtual teams. Getting the teams to actually work as a team is the greatest challenge."

"Time constraints—students' desires and motivations impede virtual team work."

"My experience has been that often there is one person who does not pull his weight. This can be frustrating for the other team members. Also, if the group is academically heterogeneous, the assignments must be designed to help each student access the curriculum at an appropriate level."

"Getting students comfortable with constructive feedback is an issue. They're so concerned with offending their peers on virtual teams that communication becomes a huge issue."

"My new students to online learning are very challenged as it is, and working in virtual teams presents more challenges; they are unprepared to collaborate with others."

"Slackers and free riders, lack of communication, inability to set due dates—for example, if everyone can wait until Saturday to participate, some will. That does not work for virtual teams."

See the Appendix for more survey results from professionals on virtual teams.

CHAPTER 6: REVIEW

The Virtual Team Global Business Model can be adapted to higher education. *Instructional designers* take on the role management serves in the business environment. ISDs design the course, set goals, objectives, and create tasks—in this application, assignments—following the VTML. ISDs meet with instructors to discuss the assignments and expectations during Communication Phase 1. This should be a synchronous meeting or webinar if the ISD is meeting with several instructors to review the course design. *Instructors* take on the project manager or team leader role defined by the VTML. They are responsible for administering the Virtual Team Skills Assessment and assigning students to teams. The instructors ultimately facilitate the teams and assign a student VTG to help collect students' assignment submissions. Unlike the business environment, the role of *student virtual team guides* doesn't involve ensuring that all the work is completed. They are responsible for guiding the team, organizing meetings, and compiling the team members' task submissions into one document for grading. Finally, the *students* are the virtual team members who collaborate to complete their assignments.

The VTML provides a framework for the preparation and organization of virtual teams to promote the quality of assessments. Following the VTML can improve student participation and offer defined expectations. Using the VTML as a guide for virtual teams in higher education helps to promote the active involvement of instructors, ensures accountability among all parties, and makes it easier to manage conflict.

CHAPTER 7

DETERMINING WHAT WORKS FOR VIRTUAL TEAMS

Finding out what works for virtual teams requires a lot of practice. Distance education and working collaboratively have become more prevalent for a variety of reasons, ranging from cost-effectiveness to using geographically dispersed employees' skills in a more manageable way. Learning how to manage teams that are not housed together in a brick-and-mortar venue requires effort and guidance. Management need the tools and resources to set the teams up and oversee them once they begin their projects. This entails being involved in the virtual teams every step of the way through active communication, checking in consistently, offering support to the appointed leaders, and evaluating team members' needs and the success of the project. One important aspect of the Virtual Team Global Business Model, with its focus on accountability and communication, is that management provide the driving force for the entire project. They don't leave their virtual teams to work alone. Management adopt the people-driven philosophy underpinning the VTML, not a technology-driven philosophy.

Following the VTML:

- Managers do not assume that employees already know how to work at a distance.
- Managers do not assume that employees already understand how to navigate the technology required.
- Managers do not assume that employees are already familiar with the conflict resolution strategies required to combat any pettiness among team members for the good of the project and the company.

The topics covered in this book have emphasized the need for the active involvement of managers, leaders, and team members when working on remote projects. Here is a review of the main points regarding the application of the VTML.

Chapter 1 introduced the Virtual Team Global Business Model. It discussed the overall benefits of the model, and explained how to identify and close performance gaps. Examples of these were identified in the fictional O-Span Youth e-commerce project referred to throughout the earlier chapters of book. It then covered how virtual team dynamics and substandard communication influence virtual team members and working collaboratively, and explained how performance gaps apply to all the dimensions of virtual team collaboration, including employees knowing what to expect and what they are responsible for completing on a particular project.

In addition, it defined asynchronous and synchronous communication, and explained how virtual teams can be set up using these methods. It discussed the issues involved in each of them, and how the VTML can benefit teams by stipulating the need for synchronous communication and specifying times when team members are available to work online. It introduced the concept of expectations about deliverables and the need for check-points, clarifying how the VTML can be used to organize all these elements in virtual projects. The main argument of the chapter was that the VTML offers a viable approach to developing and managing virtual teams and projects.

Chapter 2 explained management's roles in the VTML, highlighting the importance of management defining goals, objectives, and tasks. It laid out why it's important to define and communicate clear, workable goals for VTMs, teams, and the project as a whole. It emphasized the importance of management defining specific objectives and tasks to achieve the goals, and that it may be necessary to revise and edit the goals in order to do so.

It provided examples to demonstrate how objectives preview the responsibilities that need to be fulfilled. It explained tasks in detail, stressing the importance of them being action-oriented and specifying precise roles for all those involved. The chapter's main points were that management must maintain a strong presence on virtual teams, articulate the expectations for each VTM, and solicit help if necessary to define these roles and performance expectations to enable employees to be successful as distance workers.

Chapter 3 covered the role of the team leader or project manager in the VTML. It explained that a key aspect of this involves converting the tasks that have been defined into the deliverables that need to be completed, showed how simple processes such as drawing up a list of specific duties help in this, and how more detailed deliverables can then be derived depending on the complexity of the project. It gave examples of converting tasks into deliverables to clarify how this vital step should be accomplished.

It also emphasized the importance of identifying VTMs' skills, described how to conduct a Virtual Team Skills Assessment, and explored ways to build rapport among VTMs. The main point of the chapter was that team leaders or project managers have to be familiar with the various areas of the company's operations in order to create deliverables that are realistic and tailored to VTMs' skill sets.

Chapter 4 defined the roles of virtual team guides and virtual team members in the VTML. It explained that virtual team guides are responsible for dealing with many details that have a significant impact on virtual teams' progress. It explored how VTGs have to be skilled in conflict resolution and concentrate on the project's goals, objectives, and tasks in order to keep VTMs focused and avoid the team being sidetracked by pettiness, and emphasized the importance of VTGs constantly monitoring VTMs' progress on their deliverables using tools such as the Virtual Team Progress Form. It explained that these were not intended to grade employees, but to catalogue their progress and highlight any areas where improvement was necessary.

The chapter also stressed that virtual team members are the heart of the organization. They have to work consistently to meet deliverable deadlines, and to do this, they must have the tools required to do their jobs effectively. It emphasized that VTMs should not be distracted by logistical concerns, but should be able to concentrate on their tasks and collaborating effectively with their coworkers. The most important point of the chapter was that VTMs must have the support they need from management.

Chapter 5 gave a detailed explanation of the business applications of the VTML. It explored the reasons behind the growth in the use of virtual teams, including reduced travel costs, the ability to train and utilize employees in geographically dispersed locations, opportunities to garner feedback from different VTMs on a global scale for project development, and making efficient use of VTMs' skill sets.

The chapter highlighted the need for effective collaboration and introduced the concept of process standards to ensure the integrity of the project design and maintain the reputation of the company for providing high-quality goods and services. It explained that in the VTML, management are responsible for defining overall process standards, and may either set standards for its virtual teams or allow them to define their own. The main point of the chapter was that effective collaboration should be the norm for virtual teams. Anything less than that is problematic and requires management to assess any gaps that might have been overlooked and are caused issues among VTMs.

Chapter 6 explained in detail how the VTML can be applied to higher education, showing how it can be adapted to students working on group assignments at a distance. It argued that too often when virtual teamwork is part of the curriculum, students receive little or no guidance about how to collaborate on class assignments, and have no say in the roles they are allocated in virtual teams. It explained the role of instructional designers in defining the course parameters and the importance of preparation to ensure that assignments are viable. It also focused on the need for instructors to maintain active engagement to help to resolve conflicts and play a strategic role in overseeing virtual teams and individual students. The chapter's main point was that students must be clear about the expectations and their roles and activities in their virtual teams, and this relies the active involvement of the instructor.

Throughout these earlier chapters, the theme has been how the VTML can be used to promote team building and conflict resolution through its focus on accountability and effective communication. The next stage is to complete the process by assessing team members' satisfaction with their project.

AN EVALUATION COMPONENT

When working with virtual teams, it is important to include an evaluation process at the conclusion of a project. This will not only enable you to determine the effectiveness of the project, but provide ideas for improvements that can be applied to future virtual team projects. As emphasized earlier, team members are the heart of the organization and its virtual team projects, so it is important to canvass their views about their overall experience. The evaluation should consist of two parts: the Program Review and the Team Experience Review.

Program Review

It is a good idea to review the overall program or project. In the Program Review, VTMs assess the flow and expectations of the project, as well as offer any suggestions for improvements to make their jobs easier within their specific disciplines, such as marketing or information technology.

Here are some suggestions for Program Review questions:

1. What are you initial thoughts about the virtual team project? (Ideas to develop in this answer could include effectiveness, appropriateness, quality, or processes.)
2. Discuss any expectations and concerns you had about this project.

3. Were process standards met? Please explain your answer.
4. What were some of the highs and lows of this project?
5. How user-friendly was the technology provided for the project?
6. Did you have any concerns about the project's software programs and Web-based meetings? Please list them.
7. How would you rate the quality of technical assistance and answers on a scale of 1 to 5 (1 = very poor, 5 = excellent)?
8. Do you have any suggestions of future virtual team projects for our business? Please list them.
9. Do you have any recommendations for improvements in your project area? Please list them.
10. What are your final thoughts about the virtual team project now that it is complete?

Virtual Team Experience Review

Here are some suggestions for Virtual Team Experience Review questions:

1. How did you feel about the VTG's instruction and assistance?
2. How well was the project tailored to your understanding and skills as an employee?
3. How did you feel about the duties assigned to you?
4. Were your team members responsive? Please explain your answer.
5. What could be done differently to help improve the virtual team experience?
6. What did you learn about yourself while working on this virtual team?
7. What did you learn about your coworkers while working on this virtual team?
8. How would you rate your feelings of isolation when working online during this project on a scale of 1 to 5 (1 = very isolated, 5 = not isolated at all)?
9. How would you rate your performance on the team on a scale of 1 to 5 (1 = very poor, 5 = excellent)?
10. How would you rate your overall experience on a scale of 1 to 5 (1 = very poor, 5 = excellent)?

LESSONS LEARNED

The use of virtual teams continues to grow as technology develops and more people work collaboratively at a distance. A new mode of instruction and assistance for remote workers is needed in the form of *electronic pedagogy*. Electronic pedagogy defines best practices when using technology to accomplish goals and tasks. It focuses on new approaches and skills for remote workers to make working online more effective. Electronic pedagogy is not about object-driven approaches to remote working, it is about people-driven approaches. The VTML offers ways to help manage remote workers collaborating at a distance.

Chapter 1 listed six aspects of the VTML that are critical to success when working at a distance:

1. It provides a hierarchical process for distance teamwork.
2. It specifies a clear communication process.
3. It helps to clarify process standards.
4. It sets clear goals, objectives, and tasks for participants.
5. It solidifies the expected deliverables for remote workers.
6. It can be used along with distance working software.

Let's discuss how each of these contributes to building and maintaining a viable online community of employees to promote successful virtual team outcomes.

It Provides a Hierarchal Process for Distance Teamwork

In the VTML, management initiate the hierarchical process. Team leaders or project managers have management as an information resource, and can refer to management throughout the process if there are any problems they can't deal with themselves. At the next stage in the hierarchy, VTGs have team leaders or project managers as a resource, and can enlist their assistance if any issues are beyond their abilities or knowledge. Finally, VTMs can turn to the VTGs or team leaders and project managers for assistance, as well as other VTMs.

This hierarchal structure is essential, and it must be explained clearly to employees, not only to help them solve any problems, but to impress on them that they are not alone in what can often be complex and multilayered distance projects.

It Specifies a Clear Communication Process

Clear communication and e-communication flow are pivotal to the success of virtual teams. The VTML promotes fluid communication and check-points to ensure that there are no misunderstandings and that progress is not impeded by issues that have not been communicated or resolved. Communication is the foundation of the VTML, because without a full understanding and implementation of communication methods, virtual team projects will be ineffective and the people working on them will be set up for failure.

It Helps to Define Process Standards

Process standards are the guidelines that are critical to each stage of development. Setting them is another task for management. It is important for employees to understand from the beginning that management are invested in the project, that it is considered important, that quality matters, and their efforts must be directed to achieving it. The VTML encourages management to demonstrate that they are invested, not simply paying lipservice while taking no active role. This means that VTMs are more likely to fully engage in their tasks, and not jeopardize the quality of the project due to frustration, lack of help from the management team, or because conflict issues are not being resolved.

It Sets Clear Goals, Objectives, and Tasks for Participants

In the VTML, management involvement must be consistent, especially at the beginning of the project when defining the goals, objectives, and tasks for the VTMs. This is a major effort that involves management assessing the project needs to establish the goals, objectives, and tasks that will eventually be conveyed to team leaders or project managers as deliverables. The scope of the project, its progress, and its results rely on management being clear about what they want and what they expect. This critical thinking process results in the definition of clear goals, objectives, and tasks for all participants.

It Solidifies the Expected Deliverables for Remote Workers

As explained earlier in this book, when remote workers (whether managers, employees, instructors, or students) follow the VTML, they know what is expected of them. Issues of silence or resistance and the scope for conflict can be managed rather than escalated because remote workers are clear about the deliverables. Management may set goals and have a clear idea of what they want, but unless this is conveyed clearly to VTMs, the deliverables may be totally different than what management expected. Management will do themselves, and their company, a huge favor if they ensure throughout the virtual team process that their subordinates understand what is required in terms of the project deliverables. Using check-points, Virtual Team Progress Forms, and consistent check-ins ensures that everyone is clear about the deliverables and how to communicate, and has the support required at each stage.

It Can be Used Along with Distance Working Software

Most companies will use project management software to track progress and administer working at a distance. Some companies may run their own e-room, or use online project management tools such as creativeTrack. The VTML does not conflict with this software, but dovetails with it by providing a guide to follow in establishing check-points, accountability, and communication channels.

It is important to remember that the VTML is founded on a people-driven philosophy, emphasizing that people matter, and they are simply using the technology to do their work, whether employees or students. Their voices have to be heard and their needs responded to in order to produce excellent projects when collaborating with others at a distance.

SUMMARY: USING THE VTML

The section above on "Lessons Learned" listed six elements critical to the success of working at a distance using the VTML. Several other points are also important for professional and academic success when working remotely.

The Extent of Order and Accountability

The VTML defines the extent of order and accountability for those working remotely, whether professionally or academically. Management are accountable because they initially define the protocols for those working collaboratively. Those in leadership positions are then imbued with the knowledge required to carry out their tasks and oversee the employees or students who will eventually complete the deliverables. Those working at a distance have defined rules to follow and clear points of contact if they encounter issues.

Another aspect of the VTML with regard to the extent of order and accountability is that it gives employees a clear idea of their roles and task, avoiding ambiguity about how to complete their projects when they are not in the same location as coworkers. Their common purpose is presented clearly due to the order and logical flow of the VTML.

The Extent of Critical Thinking

The most salient characteristic of using the VTML is the amount of thought and effort each phase involves. Management must exercise critical thinking, defining explicitly at the beginning the concepts, values, and tools required by their company and the delivery of the remote project. Critical thinking is not confined to management—an analytical thought process to work is required for each group involved in bringing the remote project to fruition. As this book has emphasized, team leaders or project managers, VTGs, and VTMs also have to apply critical thinking in their roles.

Some of the areas where critical thinking is needed that have been discussed in this book include timelines and expectations for project or assignment completion, time management for both autonomous and collaborative parts of the project or assignment, constructive viewpoints about the quality of deliverables, areas where synergy within the team should be assessed and improved, adhering realistically to process standards, and multiple project management for geographically dispersed projects.

The Extent of Professionals' and Students' Knowledge About Virtual Teams

This final point basically summarizes the entire reason for investing in adopting the VTML. The people-driven concept behind it has been a constant theme throughout this book—the perspective that it is the people who are working remotely, not the technology. People-driven managers understand that communication is needed, including some voice-to-voice components, when working remotely. Guessing about how to move forward with coworkers in different locations across the globe is not effective. Management should always bear in mind that VTMs must have clearly assigned responsibilities, guidelines, skill assessments, regular check-points, access to assistance, and teamwork evaluations. Those working collaboratively using technology must be well informed about how to engage actively with their coworkers, as well as how to deal with conflict. All of these topics are integral to the VTML and have been covered in this book.

The Virtual Team Global Business Model offers ways to develop skills, work effectively, and solve problems when collaborating remotely. Often, management and employees are not adept at organizing and completing projects when they are not working face-to-face with their colleagues—as demonstrated by the observations from professional and student quoted throughout the book and in the Appendix. An effective virtual team will have clearly defined goals, objectives, tasks, deliverables, and process standards.

One final point to consider is that the virtual team does not begin with the team member; the virtual team begins with management. It's essential for management to be actively involved, and this is the fundamental distinguishing principle behind the VTML. All subsequent groups in the virtual team fall into place when those in charge are well organized and have ensured that strategic communication points have been established.

APPENDIX: SURVEY RESULTS FROM PROFESSIONALS ON VIRTUAL TEAMS

Other observations from the survey responses can be found in Chapter 6. Some saw virtual teams as advantageous, some were indifferent toward them, and some saw them as disadvantageous. Unique and interesting points are highlighted in **bold**.

"I feel that as professionals, team work would be fine. However, I do not feel that students would like this. My opinion is based on the lack of success in the classroom team work."

"Students and professionals are able to see the work each other has done and practice assessing the work of others. Learning to collaborate online with contemporaries, especially as corporate America and other industries are increasingly moving towards the www."

"When properly motivated, teammates will do well to voice many opinions and positions on the issue. You will get many minds working together to accomplish a single goal, and the output is multiplied."

"In regard to professionals, it gives us an opportunity to collaborate with one another. Students are able to learn how to delegate tasks and work in cooperation with others."

"It makes up for the gap in a ground environment."

"Certainly the advantages include the team's ability to work as a team from any location along with the type of interaction that can be made.

The nice thing is that a virtual team can meet at any time without regard to distance or travel and still accomplish stated goals."

"Students will eventually seek employment and will need to be able to work on various teams."

"I believe that it is important to learn how to work with others even remotely. This is a great career skill to have."

"I think the ease of collaboration is great, but with teams in the classrooms students do not keep up with the stronger 1 or 2 team members. Few of the students do most of the work."

"For some students, it gives them an opportunity to develop leadership skills and learn how to collaborate with teammates."

"Working in virtual teams can provide students practice for working in similar teams after they graduate and start a career. Working in virtual teams can provide professionals with experience that might improve their job position or provide experience in other areas surrounding their job title."

"Our students never seem to get the hang of working in teams. The assignments are 98% of the time a flop. As far as professionals, that depends on their position at the college and the purpose of the teams. I think it's fine for trainees and administrators working on projects. I don't see a real function of it for instructors."

"Students will have options for help."

"Shows the importance of teamwork in the workplace."

"This provides real life experience."

"You will lose students who really don't like to work in virtual teams, good students don't want to depend on lazy/nonproductive classmates for their grades—if you do a good study of this, you will discover you are losing enrollments because of this factor—and thus you are losing revenues."

"This allows people to collaborate and connect to one another over a distance. Often times being online or remote can leave you feeling isolated or disconnected. Teams allow you to participate and engage in the community."

"Students will understand how to function with diverse individuals."

"At an upper level of learning virtual teams are important. At an entry level, online virtual teams are confusing and unnecessary."

"This is part of real life experience—we do not work alone—we have to learn how to work with others as a team and how to communicate effectively to complete work."

"Virtual teams allow the student to gain experience needed in many positions and companies that operate in the global environment."

"Camaraderie."

"Professionals—utilize leadership and facilitation skills; students—time management and discipline; developing leaderships skills."

"I think instructors, administrators and other professionals can improve their understanding of operations, instruction and curriculum development in teams, particularly cross-disciplinary teams. Students do learn some team skills with team assignments."

"Collaboration engenders analysis and synthesis of new ideas. It also breeds confidence."

"Team Work, Exposure to New Ideas."

"For the virtual teams to be effective, the individuals working on the teams must be prepared and willing to embrace virtual teams."

"If we are preparing our students for the world of work, we need to prepare them to work in virtual teams. This mode of work has increased and will only increase."

"Professional collaboration and cooperation."

"When students work in virtual teams in a class, they are simulating workplace situations that they may encounter in their careers."

"I think Professionals can do this, but the problem with students who are studying to be professionals, they are not prepared, nor do many of them have the necessary skills to do this. Another issue is time available for them to perform in teams."

"They get to experience a team work situation."

"I think it gives everyone a chance to bounce ideas off one another and work with fewer people than a general class discussion."

"For professionals, I think it helps us to get to know one another and learn from each other. For students, it can be the same, but I think the challenges outweigh the benefits."

"It is similar to the collaborative learning found in face-to-face classrooms."

"More ideas can be brought to the table and a sharing of a workload can occur."

"Teamwork is an important part of life. I think teamwork experience is good for students."

"It provides interaction."

"Making contributions to help out the team as in a work team capacity."

"I don't know that there are any benefits. Most of my students have not liked working in teams. Someone always feels left holding the bag."

"I see none at all. Students have conflicts, one person does seems to do more of the work (even with the individual grades), and I got tired of

having to reshuffle students from one group to another. I cannot see one benefit from them at all."

"I have worked on many committees which use virtual teams to assign tasks to the members and they work together to get the tasks completed. This is usually done in Google Docs. It is helpful to be working on a live document in which everyone is participating. I see many benefits in working in virtual teams if all the team members are motivated and there are no slackers. :) As for students, I do not see many benefits in working in this format and they become very frustrated very quickly when members are not performing adequately."

"I think that virtual teams can be beneficial to some students as some will go on to work in these sorts of teams in their future careers."

"I think if the team is purposeful and the task requires teamwork it is a good idea."

"I think it is great for professionals to share ideas and practices. Distance teams would increase the diversity of collaborative thought. Students have difficulty working in distance teams. They each have their own agendas and learning styles and some are more grade-oriented than others."

"Flexibility, I know that if I have a team that I can count on, then when I need to give them more work that makes the process easier. The same is true when I can take on more of their work when they need it. Makes everything much simpler."

"The art of collaboration."

"I think students can benefit, but find it very challenging and frustrating. Instructors/professionals can benefit from the input and ideas of others in a collaborative environment."

"Working in a virtual team helps students understand the importance of teamwork. It helps a student or professional understand although the

majority of their school success is an individual effort, there are times when a team is also part of that success."

"For professionals, it allows people to work together who might not otherwise have the chance due to distance. For students, it gives them an opportunity to work on interacting with others to reach a common goal."

"Problem solving and collaborating at a distance are practical skills in today's workplace. Being able to work with people in person on tasks is not possible or even necessary."

"Understanding how to effectively manage a virtual team will be beneficial both academically and professionally. There is an increase in tele-commuting in many offices and depending on the job, you may virtually work with people across the country on various projects."

"Shared knowledge, more ideas, get practice working on communication, & delegating tasks spreads out workload."

"The students who understand the material are able to help those who don't understand."

"Collaboration fosters better ideas and offers a multi-perspective view of the topic at hand."

"To better understand the dynamics of team assignments which they will encounter in the real world."

"One benefit is increased productivity because virtual teams often see an increase in productivity. More personal flexibility is achieved, commute time is reduced, and work is not restricted by a 9–5 work day schedule. Because there is never an off hour, teams can pick up where prior teams left off. This advantage can translate to a much faster time to develop and plan for new products and technology. Extended market opportunity is a major benefit of geographically dispersed teams due to direct access to different types of strategic company marketing ideas. Companies are able to establish their presence with their students globally without

being limited to a particular area. The ability to transfer knowledge is a great benefit of a virtual teams. Utilizing people with different types of knowledge spread out across the virtual community can be very beneficial to any company. Online meetings, remote computer access, wireless technology, and conferencing systems offer a way for participants and share in strategic planning from anywhere in the world. This benefit can enable most companies to become successful world-wide."

"One benefit would be brainstorming ideas. Brainstorming which promotes teamwork interaction."

"Teams help motivate & hold people accountable. You can learn from one another."

"Students do not get much benefit from working in teams in the virtual classroom. The accountability to participate seems invisible, there are too many social loafers in the classroom, the students who are conscientious and do a good job feel cheated by the ones who don't. These team assignments make schools look bad to students because it does not appear to students who do take the team assignments seriously that administrators are serious in holding others accountable. There is no value gained by the students who do pull their share of the load because the final submission is still dependent on their work. They might as well be doing this as an individual assignment."

"Can pool resources and expertise."

"It is important to realize that teamwork is necessary. There will always be someone who doesn't pull their weight. It is good to get practice with learning how to handle these situations."

"The opportunity for collaboration and gathering a variety of ideas and perspectives in an environment with some measure of anonymity or sense of creative freedom."

"I believe that one of the biggest benefits is learning how to communicate with one another and produce an end result."

"Prepares individuals for future working models of collaboration and sharing of information among teams on a virtual platform, especially in global professions."

"Building networks and connections with classmates and colleagues. An additional tool for determining grades within class. I've noticed that some of my student's grades improve after working as a team because they learn from each other. I mix A and C students and it diversifies the environment. Usually when putting members into team, I put them in based on their typical activity. In theory students that start at the beginning of the week get grouped together, those in the middle are grouped together, and those in the end are grouped together."

"I believe the benefits of working in virtual teams is developing good goal setting techniques, time management skills, leadership skills, as well as a chance to communicate with peers."

"It helps get ideas flowing."

"I believe understanding how to communicate in a virtual world is vital to the professional success of our students. However, I believe that virtual teams may be most effective when students are at least a year into their program. Otherwise, students are attempting to become familiar with the online learning environment while attempting to understand the additional communication skills that are necessary to meet the goals of virtual teams. Therefore, I truly believe the answer will depend on the level of the student."

"Learn to collaborate, divide responsibilities, engage in professional behaviors they can transfer to the workplace later."

"It allows peers to get together and use their critical thinking skills."

"The benefits are everyone is 'accountable,' and no one solitary person is responsible. Having the support of teammates when unsure is comforting. Additionally, it builds on one's people skills and communication skills by requiring participants to proof messages and posts, etc. ensuring true

intentions are being communicated effectively. Finally, although I feel there are more reasons; it alleviates the stress some students may feel in person if unsure about content. In other words they are more open to being their true selves because there are no 'eyes' of judgment glaring at them when they need help. Likewise for professionals."

"To learn to be sensitive to others and their input. Learn to suspend judgment."

"Professionals can help each other identify best practices and can provide support. I do not think that team assignments work with this undergraduate population."

"Good practice for students to learn to share and work in team environments."

"Feedback from peers rather than from the instructor can be beneficial."

"Students are able to learn important collaborative skills, which can benefit them in the workplace. In my writing courses, students benefit from having peer feedback, which provides them with additional comments and viewpoints outside of the instructor's point of view."

"If the team is a small number of people it is nice to get to know them better."

"There are great benefits to building an online community and support."

"Helps to create cohesiveness within the virtual classroom. Working as a team should create a sense of belonging to a group and having a good attitude toward each other."

"I personally think it is a great opportunity for both students and professionals to be exposed to new ways of thinking and solving problems."

"Forced to interact and collaborate on goals."

"Exchange of ideas."

"The benefit of having students and professionals working in virtual teams is to learn from working closely with a diverse group to achieve a common goal. Working in virtual teams can cut cost and time in completing projects as well."

"When it is not possible to meet face-to-face an organization has a wider field from which to select members."

"Working in virtual teams is a great way to learn how to work in groups. It is no secret that we are becoming a more technology based society. Moreover, working in virtual teams is great preparation for students to gain before entering the work field."

"They learn how they would work in teams of cohorts while in the field. They would learn the skills and weaknesses they would have to work with in the real world."

"It gives my students a chance to experience and hopefully overcome the challenges of group work, and it gives me the chance to collaborate with fellow instructors and bounce ideas off of them towards bettering myself as an instructor."

"The students are able to have interaction with the Instructor. In some cases, the Instructor can facilitate to assist students with preparation of team assignments."

"The extensive feedback they get."

"New technology skills teambuilding skills builds cohort closeness builds collaboration skills—important for later work."

"Benefits would be for higher level students to work in teams (400-level courses). This group would more fully understand the need for collaboration. 100–200-level students do not participate as fully."

"Not judged by appearance, freedom to speak and be heard, convenient time to work."

"Underperforming students can be 'brought up' to higher standards by working with others. Encouragement, modeling and accountability are present in virtual teams."

"Having support from your peers—learning how to work with others."

"Collaboration is what it's about. Students, and professionals, have to learn to work with other people. It's what most companies require today in the job market."

"I believe there is a strong divide between professionals and students in relation to virtual teams. From what I've experienced, students are often intimidated by teamwork because they do not like others affecting their grade. Even if you the instructor informs them that this will not be the case, most students still seem troubled by the aspect of teamwork. Professionals, on the other hand, seem to understand that teamwork is important in regards to academia."

"Virtual teams allow students to accomplish team goals (group-think) across varying time zones. Ideally, virtual teams could be used to encourage participation from shy/low-performing students."

"Benefits of collaboration."

"It is enjoyable to work online with others from various parts of the country. Students learn to cooperate, accommodate, and complete tasks online."

"I believe the premise behind teamwork is good but, as an instructor, I am relying on my students to do their fair share. Sometimes the groups come together perfectly and other times I only have one or two participants. It all depends on the student's activity level."

"How the real world works being able to work together and in teams."

"The biggest benefit to working in virtual teams is flexibility and the collaboration of skills. It is a great way to work with talented and

*experienced individuals who may not all be in the same office or city.
It also saves time from having to physically meet. A person can attend
a meeting at their desk or log into the meeting forum at any time to
contribute to the team task."*

**"Professionals can increase creativity, motivation and commitment
working on virtual teams. However, in my experience, many students in
my online classes do not do well in team situations, and the team projects
in the past have often become negative motivators. Only a few students
respond to team assignments, and of those who do, a number are often
the most talented in the class. When these most talented students find
that few of their classmates are doing teamwork and that the talented
students are the ones who are then burdened with most of the work, the
activity has a negative impact. I believe our recent decision to eliminate
the team projects from some classes are positive steps toward increased
and positive student motivation."**

*"On certain concrete issues, I think it could be beneficial; however in an
English classroom, it could be a problem."*

"Increase communication and cohesiveness."

"I do not think that it is beneficial for students to work in virtual teams."

*"This is a mixed bag thing for students. It is supposed to assist them
in working together, and yet many assume it is their opportunity to not
participate at all, expecting others to pick up the slack. It creates more
tension in the online classroom than any other activity."*

"Networking/Collaboration Skill Development."

**"I think that for students that are not in a specific 'group' class
(i.e. small group communication), there aren't enough benefits to
outweigh the drawbacks of working in teams. For professionals, I think
a benefit is to learn to let others give their input and do work while
balancing that with your own contribution."**

"For professionals, it's good for collaboration. I find that most students don't like it or get much out of it."

"Teamwork helps to build a sense of community and is a way to come up with many different ways to solve a problem or accomplish an objective."

"It encourages student responsibility and interaction."

"They learn to be responsible for their own part in the group."

"Collaboration and communication open up. There is more sharing opportunities which bring multiple benefits to the classroom."

"Doing so provides collegiality and collaboration, problem solving and patience, and critical thinking skills. These are important aspects in and outside of the classroom."

"I think the main thing is collaboration."

"It teaches them collaboration, communication, and holds them accountable for their portion of the assignment."

"Building teamwork skills and communication skills."

"Building a sense of community. ... Learning to appreciate diverse views and perspectives. ... Working towards the same goal(s). ... Sharing common ground."

"They share professional / work experience."

"It fosters a sense of community which is so important to distance learning. My students, for the most part, quickly become like a family working toward a common goal. I monitor student teamwork closely to deal with any issues immediately if a problem arises, but for the most part, I appreciate the cooperation and accomplishment teamwork adds to the classroom."

"Professionals often have demanding schedules and working in virtual settings allows for them to work at their own pace within a reasonable amount of time."

"Feeling of connection, opportunities to learn from each other, team skills."

"They develop skills in collaboration and communication."

"Collaborative learning is a valuable tool. Students often learn more by realizing they have something to teach each other."

"It is the way the world is going."

"It provides an opportunity for students to interact and collaborate with one another. There is little interaction amongst students in our online environment and so this is a chance for them to get to know one another and work together to complete a task."

"More diversity within feedback and a stronger sense of working together for a shared goal that may not otherwise be present within an online setting."

"Getting to know one another—co-workers."

"Students learn how to work with people of varying backgrounds and meet deadlines."

"Some projects and decisions require collaboration. Being able to work with individuals via electronic tools is and will remain an important skill. With that said, having students work in a discussion and respond to each other is a type of team collaboration. Assigning an arbitrary discussion with fewer individuals does not necessary improve virtual team communication skills. A better idea might be a mock meeting. Person A is the Sheriff, person B a probation officer, etc. Students have to play out their role to come up with a real world solution."

"It is the wave of the future in many workplaces."

"Collaborative work increases interaction and decreases a sense of isolation in an online environment. It also provides the opportunity for peer review of work and ultimately, the end product can be a better one if everyone participates."

"The collaboration aspect is great for professionals and students who understand the importance of team work. It can be beneficial to learn from others' perspectives. Online learning offers a chance for students to learn from others across the globe."

"Students will have to work with others in a job setting. I think it helps to prepare them for working in groups. They also have to learn what to do when someone doesn't pull their weight in a team. I think it is a valuable experience."

"It provides a flexibility and availability for students and professionals. A number of students would not be able to attend traditional brick and mortar schools because of location, family and/or work issues, etc. The virtual classroom opens up a number of opportunities for them. For professionals, virtual teams broader their base of connections with other professionals."

"It is applicable to real life."

"The primary benefit is the sharing of knowledge. In a traditional team meeting, words are lost or overlooked during the process of the meeting. In a virtual meeting, all information is recorded and able to be addressed asynchronously. More information is shared in virtual teams."

"The exchange of ideas thanks to multiple perspectives."

"The sharing of information and ideas is beneficial."

"It teaches the students or professionals how to communicate and how to collaborate in order to accomplish the task at hand."

"I believe that students that are diligent and prepared do very well in the virtual team environment."

"The reality is that we are now becoming more of a global workforce and virtual teams will be a part of that more often than not. We need to be preparing our students for this fact, even if they don't like it."

"I'm not sold on the benefits in an online format. From my experience, one or two team members end up carrying the weight of the entire team, which causes more problems than it solves."

"Coordination—who leads, old habits—trying to meet or call or chat for all things. Feeling of someone else determines my grade."

"They don't work, too much conflict, good students end up doing all the work, and instructors spend too much time reading all of the complaints from students. Let students be responsible for their own work, online students are challenged enough, don't give them one more obstacle to discourage them."

"There is always at least one person if not more who do not participate or pull their own weight. One person may be forced to 'row the entire boat by themselves.' A student who is an A student may get extremely frustrated if not working with other A students. Since the terms are shorter than semester length and students don't always know each other from term to term, it is harder to build that 'bonding' that comes with being in person."

"Not everyone is reliable, and in the virtual world it is too hard to ensure your teammates participate. Frustration is high in teams."

"Non-participating members, failure of someone to step up and assume the leadership position."

"Time, work, no ability to select the team as a student, it is forced participation. Many students have dis-enrolled from other colleges due to team mandating."

"People seem to be more bold and abrasive online compared to on-ground. This increases the usual friction caused by wanting to be a big fish in a little team pond."

"People not having an organized time schedule to allow for it. People not having a high tech skill level to use the tools necessary for teams at a distance."

"Some (most, in my experience) students don't participate at all. As usually happens in any group exercise, one person does most or all of the work. The stronger students don't get much out of the exercise other than lots of extra work."

"People working with different deadlines."

"One student typically wants an A and does or redoes all the others and submits it to get an A. Many students do not log in until Saturday to do any weekly work."

"Both students and professionals need to learn how to work collaboratively. How to work on a team needs to be taught."

"Schedules sometimes cause conflict. Meeting deadlines for all can be a challenge to many students. This is best addressed by setting clear expectations and seeking individual acceptance from each in the team."

"The only challenge is for the participant to be comfortable with the technology being used."

"For the students, I see that taking ownership is an issue."

"Schedule. Not everyone will be putting the same effort in at the same time and this can be frustrating to the team."

"If all teammates do not participate, it puts a strain on the group."

"Time. There are different time zones, schedules, people's lives, it requires an increasingly sophisticated level of communication but these are skills that can be utilized in multiple arenas."

"Staying motivated. In my experience, online students are NOT motivated enough to handle teamwork assignments. In my courses, the teamwork assignments were, without fail, the least participated in and lowest scoring assignments of the entire course. I'd have to imagine most online instructors or professionals would only do the bare minimum in a teamwork assignment."

"I do not see the value in virtual teamwork."

"It can be difficult when not all team members are invested or feel prepared."

"Team members who do not actively participate. Inability to contact via phone to prod participation."

"In my experience, it is getting members of the team together virtually online and for each member to contribute equally to the team."

"Having all team members participate on the same time line and contributing at the same level is challenging and frustrating when a student's grade depends on it."

"Students often do not know how to work on a virtual team. Some students will simply allow one of the other teammates to do their part."

"Some of the challenges are that many of the students are not prepared to work in teams at this point in their learning career. This can be frustrating to them. Learning teams are easier when there is at least some form of a synchronous component."

"Teamwork is not a good idea for first quarter students. This should be introduced after students have learned Netiquette, good grammar and APA writing skills."

"I found when working in a virtual team that communication can be challenging, including everyone on the team (especially those absent at the start of the team work), and completing the task in a timely manner. This is not only frustrating for those participating in the team but it holds especially true for the person facilitating the virtual team."

"Rarely does everyone put a similar amount of effort into the work. This is true in f2f teams as well, but in the virtual word, there is no f2f accountability, so my experience shows that one or two people (usually me) end up doing all of the work."

"Getting everyone on the same page."

"It is not possible to motivate all members of the group to do their share of work."

"Not all people participating."

"The main challenge I see is having limited time. Not being able to get up and talk to someone real quick about an issue or concern makes collaboration a little difficult. It is easier to assess progress and competency in person."

"Some individuals feel intimidated."

"Participation and understanding of the needs and tasks are challenges. Specific guidelines must be set and met to be successful."

"It's hard when the students can't count on the other students to show up. That's why I would put all non-participating students on one team and move them into an active team if they show up. Students seem to be unaware of how much they have to lose by not participating in the team—as if they will receive points no matter what. The incentive to participate is not strong enough for the majority of the students in an intro level class."

"Understanding computer programs and the time aspects."

"Not everyone pulls his/her weight; not everyone is good at time management; not everyone has the same level of skills."

"Time zones, lack of participation, slow responses, do not meet deadlines, imbalance in who completes and submits assigned outcomes."

"Getting all the members involved."

"Lack of participation from team members; one person always ends up with the most work; unmotivated members lack of time management."

"Students are not equipped to work in teams as many of them don't have the skills to manage personality differences via distance nor the sense of urgency or commitment to the team, especially when they work with others with whom they have no long-term connection. These are challenges for professionals, as well, but not to the same degree."

"My students are barely able to navigate the classroom and submit assignments. Many never find the teamwork area and are intimidated by the whole process. Only about 10% of students participate and the meaning and purpose is therefore lost on them."

"Getting buy-in from the team members and time zone differences in coordinating the teams create challenges."

"In general higher education has failed to teach students how to work in true teams, much less virtual teams as we have never done it. 99% of my fellow students claimed teams did not work and they had never had a positive experience in teams. When probed they had group work and committee experience and that is not team, much less virtual team. Researchers are still trying to determine how to make virtual teams as effective as high performing work teams which interact face to face. I am doing my dissertation on this and have worked with over 2000 teams to date. I have worked with virtual teams since the late 90s. I have never worked with a team in higher education, although I have worked on many called 'team.' There is a formula for team effectiveness and communication skills are a large part of that formula.

Although there are introductory courses in communication; there are few in-depth courses. I have had three doctoral level courses involving team and they were very disappointing when compared to the reality of what is occurring in the workplace."

"Some students do not like working in teams. And some students do not participate with their teams, making it difficult for other team members to get the assignments done."

"With students from all over the country and different schedules, it will be difficult to find a time available during the week. Also most adjunct instructors have full time jobs."

"Unfortunately the large majority of the time students do not share responsibility and one or two end up carrying the team."

"Some students complain that they end up doing more work than other students, who sort of piggy back their way into a good grade they didn't really deserve."

SOURCES AND CONTACTS

Joseph Grenny, co-author of the *New York Times* best-seller *Crucial Conversations*, www.vitalsmarts.com.

Maysa Hawwash, Director of Talent Management Solutions at Drake International, 320 Bay Street, Suite 1700, Toronto, ON, M5H 4A6, telephone (+1) 416 216 1067 or 1 800 GO DRAKE, fax (+1) 416 216 1109, email mhawwash@na.drakeintl.com.

Imaad Mahfooz, Director of Chronos Consulting, www.chronosconsulting.org, mobile (+1) 713 817 1748, landline (+1) 832 239 5044.

Susan Wright-Boucher, Canadian recruitment and staffing industry professional, www.linkedin.com/in/susanwrightboucher.

INDEX

For Product Safety Concerns and Information please contact our EU
representative GPSR@taylorandfrancis.com
Taylor & Francis Verlag GmbH, Kaufingerstraße 24, 80331 München, Germany